Economics History on Barter System

S.A.U. Haque

Copyright

First Printing, 2025

publishingfirm@gmail.com

Disclaimer: This book is free from AI use. The cover was designed in Microsoft Publisher

Disclaimer: This book is an independently produced work by the author and has no affiliation with any board or organization. Content referencing historical, cultural, or economic entities is used under nominative fair use for educational purposes.

Contents

Beyond the Absence of Money: Defining and Theorizing Barter

Beyond the Textbook Label: Seeing Barter with Fresh Eyes

Think about the word "barter." What pops into your head? Maybe dusty textbook images of cavemen swapping rocks? That's often where we start, thanks to a definition that feels a bit... well, negative.

The "Empty Space" View: Barter as Just 'No Money'

Often, we're told barter is simply "trading without cash." Like defining silence only as the absence of noise. This view, popular in basic economics (think Mankiw's primers), paints barter as the awkward phase before money swooped in like a superhero. Its big villain? The "double coincidence of wants" – that frustrating hunt for someone who has the berries you need and wants the spearhead you made (a problem highlighted way back by Jevons).

Looking through this lens, history becomes a simple ladder: clumsy barter at the bottom, efficient money at the top. Societies without coins look... less evolved, struggling until they figured out currency. We imagine a whole "Age of Barter," even though, as thinkers like David Graeber pointed out in Debt, finding entire economies running purely on strangers swapping item-for-item is like searching for a historical unicorn. What anthropologists actually found were intricate webs of IOUs, favors, gifts, and community obligations – far richer and more complex than simple A-for-B trades. Defining barter as just "no money" flattens this reality, making the past seem less sophisticated than it truly was.

The "What It Actually Is" View: Barter as Connection and Directness

Now, let's switch lenses. What if we define barter by what it is, not just what it lacks? This perspective, often found in anthropology and sociology (think Polanyi or Mauss), sees something different. It sees:

Directness: It's you and me, trading this for that. No abstract middleman.

Reciprocity: An understanding, sometimes immediate, sometimes building over time, that we're in this exchange together. It can feel like a handshake, building trust and social bonds.

Tangibility: Often, it's about real stuff – goods, skills, favors – meeting concrete needs.

Suddenly, barter isn't just a clunky relic. It's a socially embedded act, woven into the fabric of relationships, as Polanyi argued. It's not just about the things exchanged, but the relationship between the exchangers, echoing Marcel Mauss's ideas on the power of the gift.

Through this lens, history looks different. Instead of inefficiency, we might see social glue, clever ways to manage risk when currency is unstable, or targeted swaps that get specific needs met beautifully. Anthropologists (like Humphrey & Hugh-Jones) show us communities cleverly using barter alongside money or credit, choosing the best tool for the job. It's not primitive; it's practical and socially savvy.

Barter Isn't Dead, It Just Changed Clothes

If barter was only "no money," it'd be irrelevant today, right? But the "what it is" view shows us why it's alive and kicking:

Skyscrapers Trading Favors (B2B Barter): Huge corporate networks (check out IRTA) let businesses swap millions in goods and services – excess hotel rooms for advertising, printing services for web design. They might use internal "trade credits," but the core idea is direct, need-based exchange without cash changing hands. That's the positive definition in action.

Neighbors Helping Neighbors (Community Swaps): Think local skill shares (LETS) or time banks. You design a logo for the baker down the street; they keep you supplied with sourdough. It's direct, builds community, and bypasses the need for cash – pure reciprocity and tangible exchange.

When Money Fails (Crisis Economies): Remember Argentina's crisis around 2001? Barter clubs (clubes de trueque) exploded. Millions swapped goods and services directly because the formal money system had crumbled. This wasn't "going backward"; it was human ingenuity finding a resilient way to meet needs directly when the abstract system failed.

The Lens Is the Story

So, how we define barter isn't just wordplay. Defining it merely as money's absence gives us a narrow, slightly condescending view of the past and blinds us to its powerful presence today.

Defining it by its inherent qualities – its directness, its potential for connection, its grounding in tangible needs –

paints a richer, truer picture. It reveals the complexity of past economies and unlocks our understanding of why swapping and direct exchange remain vital, adaptable human strategies, even in our hyper-monetized world. The glasses we choose to wear determine the world we see.

That Old Story About Barter? It's Missing the Human Spark.

You know the one. Economists pull it out like a favourite parlor trick: imagine poor old Ug the Caveman trying to trade his mammoth haunch. He desperately needs flint for his axe, but everyone he meets either has flint but wants berries, or wants mammoth but only has spare loincloths. This nightmare of finding the exact right person at the exact right time – the "Double Coincidence of Wants" – is painted as the great villain of pre-money life. Then, ta-da! Money arrives like a superhero, slashing through the red tape, letting Ug sell his mammoth to anyone and buy flint from someone else. Simple. Elegant. Solved.

It's a neat tale, told by smart folks like Jevons and Menger back in the day. And honestly, it's great for teaching Econ 101 – it perfectly shows why money is handy stuff (you can spend it anywhere, price things easily, save it up).

But... Did We Ever Really Live Like That?

Here's where it gets interesting. When anthropologists – the explorers of human culture like Malinowski hanging out with Trobriand Islanders, or Mauss pondering the power of a simple gift – actually looked at how people exchanged things before coins jingled in pockets, they found something... different. Richer. More human.

They saw intricate dances of gift-giving, complex webs of "I owe you one," ceremonies like the Kula ring where precious items travelled vast distances, building relationships, not just balancing books. Think less awkward swapping between strangers, more vibrant community interactions humming with reciprocity and obligation.

Then comes someone like David Graeber, digging through 5,000 years of history, and he basically throws down the gauntlet. His message? Forget the idea that spot-barter was the default. Long before kings stamped their faces on metal, people operated on credit. "I'll give you this grain now, you help me build my roof next season." These weren't cold calculations; they were logged in community memory, maybe scratched onto tally sticks, woven into the very fabric of trust and social life. These systems neatly sidestepped that whole "double coincidence" headache. You didn't need an immediate perfect match; you needed social trust.

Finding actual, historical societies dominated by the kind of anonymous, instant barter the economists imagined? It's surprisingly tough. Barter happened, sure, but often between different tribes, between strangers at the edges of communities, or maybe when established systems collapsed – not usually as the everyday glue holding a village together.

So, If Not Just the 'Matching Problem', What Were the Real Roadblocks?

Maybe the "Double Coincidence" isn't the main character in this story, but just one member of a whole troublesome gang called "Transaction Costs." Think of these as all the little (and big) frictions that make exchange difficult:

The "How Much Is It Worth?" Headache: Okay, you have chickens, I have an axe. How many chickens is an axe worth? Today? Tomorrow? What if your chickens are scrawny? Establishing fair, consistent value without a common measuring stick (like dollars or shells) is a huge puzzle.

The Trust Factor & Dodgy Deals: Is that grain truly dry? Is this spearhead properly hardened? Without quality control or a way to know who you're dealing with, barter is risky. You need trust, strong community rules, or a way to verify quality – things money, especially state-backed coins, later helped standardize. How do you enforce promises in a world without courts? Social shame worked wonders in tight-knit groups, but less so with strangers.

The Awkwardness Problem: Try paying for a handful of berries with a live cow. Some things just don't divide easily, and lugging bulky goods around is a pain. Money, being portable and divisible, is just plain convenient.

Echoes in Our Modern World

This isn't just ancient history. Look around:

Online Barter Clubs: Businesses swap services today, but often use "trade credits" – a private kind of money within their network – because direct, double-coincidence swaps are still too clunky. They still wrestle with valuing different services fairly.

Community Favors & ROSCAs: Think of neighbourhood babysitting circles or informal savings clubs (ROSCAs) in developing nations. These run on intricate systems of trust and mutual support, bypassing banks and formal money by relying on social glue to overcome exchange hurdles.

Crypto Dreams & Digital Dilemmas: Cryptocurrencies and peer-to-peer lending try to cut out middlemen, reducing some costs. But guess what? They face ghostly versions of the same old problems: establishing stable value (measurement!), ensuring security and trust (enforcement!), and making it easy for people to actually use (the matching/usability challenge).

The Takeaway: A Richer Story

So, that "Double Coincidence of Wants"? It's not wrong, it's just... incomplete. It's like a brilliantly simple sketch of one tree, mistaken for the entire, complex forest of human exchange. It remains a powerful idea for understanding one reason money is so useful.

But the real story of how we got from swapping goods to digital cash is far richer, messier, and more deeply rooted in human relationships, trust, ingenuity, and the ongoing struggle to overcome all sorts of practical hurdles. It's a story where credit, gifts, and community bonds played starring roles long before the first coin was ever minted. The DCW is a chapter, not the whole epic.

Beyond the Simple Swap: Why Barter Isn't Just Child's Play

That first image of barter – trading your apple for my orange – feels so clean, so fundamentally fair. It taps into something primal, a directness we sometimes crave in our complex world. But picture trying to build a life, a community, let alone a civilization, on just simple swaps. Suddenly, that charming simplicity reveals a web of frustrating, tangled knots.

Thinkers like Jevons, staring hard at this idea, saw the cracks immediately. They weren't just being theoretical buzzkills; they were pointing out the real-world headaches:

The "Cosmic Coincidence" Problem: Forget finding one person who wants your extra chickens. You need someone who specifically wants chickens right now, and who also happens to have the exact thing you need (say, a sturdy pair of boots), and is willing to trade at that moment. It's like trying to align planets! The more specialized we get ("I need a left-handed widget sharpener!"), the more impossible this cosmic alignment becomes. It chokes the very possibility of exchange.

The "How Many Chickens is a Song Worth?" Dilemma: Without dollars or pesos acting as a universal measuring stick, value becomes a slippery ghost. Is your handcrafted pot worth five bushels of my grain, or ten? What about compared to helping me fix my roof? Every single trade demands a fresh, potentially exhausting, negotiation. Imagine the sheer time wasted haggling over whether three fish equals one blanket today, when yesterday it might have been four!

The "You Can't Have Half a Cow" Conundrum: Need just a little bit of something valuable? Tough luck if the thing you're trading is, well, alive and whole. You can't exactly offer Bessie's hind leg if you only need a small sack of flour. Barter struggles desperately with making change, shutting down countless small, necessary transactions.

The "IOU... What Exactly?" Uncertainty: Promises are tricky when value is fluid. How do I borrow goods today and promise repayment later? What if the grain I promise spoils, or the specific tool I owe you isn't needed when payment's due? Building credit, that essential lubricant of any thriving economy, becomes a gamble based on shifting needs and potentially rotting collateral.

The Burden of Wealth: Forget bank accounts. In pure barter, your wealth is your stuff. Apples rot, pottery breaks, lumber needs storing, livestock needs feeding. Saving for the future means piling up physical goods, hoping they last and praying you don't need a bigger barn every year. It's cumbersome, risky, and deeply impractical.

But Humans Are Cleverer Than Theory: The Great Workarounds

Here's where the story gets truly interesting. While economists mapped out these very real roadblocks, actual humans on the ground rarely, if ever, let themselves be completely trapped by a "pure" barter system. We're too resourceful, too social for that! History and anthropology paint a vibrant picture of adaptation:

The Power of the Tab: Long before coins jingled, communities ran on intricate systems of favors, memory, and social debt. Think of it as a village-wide "tab." David Graeber argued compellingly that these webs of IOUs and mutual obligation often came first. You'd give your neighbor grain, knowing they'd "owe you one" – maybe help with the harvest, share a catch, or offer something else entirely down the line. It wasn't cold calculation; it was trust, reputation, and the social glue holding communities together. This elegant social technology sidestepped the need for perfect timing and exact matches in every single exchange.

"Good Enough" Money: Necessity birthed invention. People figured out that some goods were just more useful for trading than others. Things that were desirable, durable, easy to carry, divisible, and relatively uniform started acting like proto-money. Think gleaming cowrie shells passed along trade routes, salt bars used to pay Roman soldiers (where "salary" comes from!), cacao beans in Mesoamerica, or standardized bundles of grain. These weren't cash as we know it, but they were crucial stepping stones, making trade smoother by providing a more common denominator.

It's Not Just Business, It's Personal (and Social): Ever heard of the Kula ring or potlatch ceremonies? These weren't just about swapping stuff; they were elaborate dances of gift-giving, status building, and forging alliances. The exchange of goods was wrapped up in social meaning, creating obligations and strengthening bonds in ways that strict, immediate barter never could. Precise valuation often took a backseat to the relationship itself.

The Art of the Haggle and "Good Enough": Even in direct trades, rigid calculations weren't always king. Negotiation, approximation ("Yeah, that looks about right"), and the flexibility born from knowing the person you're trading with allowed for exchanges that might look messy on paper but worked perfectly well in context.

Barter's Ghost in the Modern Machine

This age-old tension between barter's limits and our knack for adaptation isn't just history. It echoes today:

High-Tech Swapping: Businesses haven't ditched barter; they've turbocharged it. Huge networks like IRTA use digital "trade credits" (like barter dollars) and sophisticated online platforms to instantly match businesses with complementary needs. They've essentially solved the coincidence, valuation, and storage problems using technology, facilitating billions in trade.

When Money Fails: Watch what happens in severe economic crises. When hyperinflation makes currency worthless, people instinctively revert. Informal barter networks spring up – trading food for fuel, skills for goods. It's inefficient, born of desperation, and highlights the very real problems barter presents, but it's also a testament to its raw resilience as a fallback.

Local Loops: Community-based LETS systems create their own internal credits, deliberately sidestepping national currency to foster local exchange and mutual support, tackling the classic barter challenges on a smaller, trust-based scale.

The Takeaway?

The economists' critique of pure barter is dead-on – it's a system riddled with inefficiencies that would stifle complex economies. But the human story isn't about being stifled. It's a richer, more dynamic narrative of constant, creative adaptation. We built systems of trust, invented intermediate currencies, wove exchange into our social fabric, and now leverage technology to make sophisticated barter work on a global scale. The "pure barter" world is a useful thought experiment, but the real world has always been messier, more ingenious, and far more fascinating. We didn't just face the limitations; we danced around them.

The Ghost in the Economic Machine: Why Barter Haunts Our Understanding of Money

Trading your hand-knitted scarf for a bag of your neighbor's prize-winning tomatoes – it feels like the most natural economic act imaginable, doesn't it? Almost primal. Yet, this seemingly simple swap, barter, has been poked, prodded, praised, and dismissed by economic thinkers for centuries, becoming a surprisingly controversial character in the story of how we get what we need.

Act I: The Awkward First Step (According to Smith)

Picture Adam Smith, the granddaddy of modern economics, observing the hustle and bustle. He saw in us this deep urge, this "propensity...to truck, barter, and exchange." It's just in us, he thought. But, like a clumsy first dance, he saw barter as inherently awkward. Its fatal flaw? The dreaded "double coincidence of wants." You have the scarf, they have the tomatoes. Easy. But what if they don't want a scarf? You're stuck, wandering the marketplace, hoping to find that one person who has what you crave and craves what you possess. It's exhausting! For Smith and his classical crew, this inefficiency was the cue for money to enter stage left – the smooth, universally desired lubricant that greased the wheels of commerce, letting everyone specialize and trade with ease. (Though, whisper archaeologists and anthropologists, sometimes money snuck in for messier reasons, like paying off debts or tribute, not just to make shopping easier).

Act II: Marx Enters – Barter, Chains, and Seeing Clearly

Karl Marx peered at barter through a different lens, one focused on power and the hidden mechanics of society. He wasn't nostalgic for it, but he saw it as something direct. Trading Commodity-for-Money-for-Commodity (C-M-C) was about getting something useful. Simple enough. But then, Marx argued, came capitalism's relentless engine: Money-buys-Commodity-to-make-More-Money (M-C-M'). Suddenly, the goal wasn't just getting useful stuff; it was endless accumulation. Money, in this view, became a kind of veil, obscuring the real human relationships, the sweat and toil, behind the goods. Barter, while perhaps clunky, didn't hide the social reality in the same way. For Marx, ditching barter wasn't just about efficiency; it was part of the journey towards exploitation and our strange modern habit of treating goods as if they have magical lives of their own ("commodity fetishism").

Act III: The Theorist's Sketchpad (Neoclassical Dreams)

Jump forward, and you find economists using barter like a theoretical sandbox. Think of those clean, elegant diagrams (hello, Edgeworth Box!) in textbooks. They often start with two people and two goods, figuring out how a simple swap could make both better off. It's a useful starting point, a way to build complex models of monetary economies step-by-step. It's less about what actually happened in history and more about proving, on paper, why having money makes the giant, complex dance of a modern economy work so much more smoothly than a world filled only with barterers desperately seeking that "double coincidence."

Act IV: The Social Network (Institutional Insights)

"Hold on!" said another group, the Institutionalists. "You're missing the human element!" They argued that barter isn't just about overcoming logistical hurdles; it's deeply woven into the fabric of society. It runs on trust, reputation, shared history, and community rules. Think about swapping favors with a neighbor – it works because you know them, you trust them, and there are unspoken rules. From this angle, barter isn't just some primitive relic. It's a social technology that can thrive when the conditions are right, sometimes existing happily alongside cash, especially in tight-knit groups or specific situations where that social glue is strong.

Barter's Encore: Still Relevant in a World Awash with Cash?

And here's the twist: barter never really left the stage.

When Money Fails: Ask Argentinians about the clubes de trueque after their economy crashed in 2001. Millions jumped into organized barter networks, swapping everything from haircuts to plumbing services, just to survive when the peso became worthless. Barter became a lifeline.

Corporate Swapping: Think barter is just for small-fry? Think again. There's a multi-billion dollar global industry where big companies trade unsold hotel rooms for advertising space, swap excess inventory for raw materials, all through sophisticated B2B barter exchanges. It's a strategic tool, not a primitive fallback.

Digital & Community Trades: Look online! Facebook Marketplace, Craigslist, dedicated swapping sites – they're buzzing with cashless trades. And think about Time Banks or Local Exchange Trading Systems (LETS), where people trade hours of work or skills based on mutual credit and community trust, operating on principles closer to those Institutionalist ideas.

The Curtain Call:

So, the story of barter in economic thought isn't a simple tale of an inefficient system gracefully exiting for money. It's been cast as the clumsy ancestor, the transparent-but-limited alternative, the useful theoretical sketch, and the trust-based social glue. Its stubborn refusal to disappear, popping up in crises, corporate boardrooms, and online communities, tells us that this ancient way of exchanging value is far more complex, resilient, and deeply human than the simplest economic models might suggest. It's a ghost that still walks, reminding us that economies are built not just on currency, but on connection, ingenuity, and trust.

Echoes from Deep History: Pre-Monetary Exchange Before States

Echoes in Stone and Shell: Touching the World of Our Ancestors

Imagine standing on a windswept plain thousands upon thousands of years ago. The world is vast, untamed, known only through the tracks of animals and the whispers of the wind. Yet, even here, connections are being forged, threads of interaction stretching across landscapes we can barely comprehend today. Forget stock markets and shipping lanes; this is the dawn of human networking, written not in ledgers, but in the very materials that shaped survival and sparked wonder.

Archaeologists today are like listeners pressing their ears to the earth, trying to catch the faint, ghostly trails left by our Palaeolithic and Neolithic forebears. These aren't loud declarations, but subtle clues: a piece of stone far from its mountain home, a seashell resting miles from any ocean. These misplaced treasures are our windows into a world where 'value' wasn't about coin, but perhaps about survival, connection, beauty, or belief.

Whispers from the Ice Age (Palaeolithic)

Picture the world of the hunter-gatherers, a life lived on the move, attuned to the rhythms of nature. Survival often hinged on having the right tools. That meant finding stone – flint, chert – that would fracture just so, yielding a life-saving edge. And they knew where the good stuff was. We find tools crafted from specific, high-quality stone hundreds of kilometres from their geological birthplace, scattered across ancient European campsites. How did they get there? Modern science, like a fingerprint kit for rocks (using X-Ray Fluorescence or isotopic analysis), can pinpoint the exact quarry. It tells us where, but the how and why remain tantalizingly open.

Think of obsidian, that sharp, volcanic glass. Even in these deep Palaeolithic times, pieces occasionally made long treks, hinting at early exchange, though its real heyday came later. Or imagine finding delicate Nassarius sea shells, maybe pierced for stringing, deep inland in places like Blombos Cave, South Africa, over 75,000 years ago! Were they carried by nomadic groups, souvenirs of a coastal visit? Or were they passed hand-to-hand, person-to-person, tiny tokens solidifying unseen social bonds across the miles?

And then there's ochre. This earthy pigment, in shades of red, yellow, and brown, wasn't just colourful dirt. It was paint for bodies, for cave walls, for rituals we can only guess at. By tracing the unique chemical signatures of ochre found at ancient sites, we've uncovered vast "ochre routes" in southern Africa during the Middle Stone Age. People were deliberately seeking out, carrying, and perhaps sharing this symbolic substance far beyond their immediate campsites. It hints at a world rich with meaning, art, and shared identity.

New Connections in a Changing World (Neolithic)

Fast forward to the Neolithic, when the rhythm of life began to change. People started settling down, cultivating land, building villages. This didn't stop the flow of materials; if anything, it intensified it, creating new hubs and reasons for connection.

Obsidian exploded onto the scene. At places like Çatalhöyük in Turkey, a bustling town nearly 9,000 years ago, archaeologists found staggering amounts of obsidian flakes and tools. Scientific analysis shows most of it came from volcanoes over 200 kilometres away! This wasn't just about making sharp knives; the sheer quantity suggests obsidian had become something more – maybe a status symbol, a vital trade good, or imbued with spiritual significance.

Imagine exquisitely polished stone axes, crafted from jadeite mined high in the Italian Alps. These weren't your everyday chopping tools; they were often impossibly beautiful, smooth, and seemingly impractical for hard labour. Yet, these "ceremonial" axes travelled astonishing distances, turning up in Neolithic graves and hoards as far away as Britain and Denmark. Passed perhaps from leader to leader, generation to generation, they likely weren't 'bought' but gifted, cementing alliances, marking status, carrying stories across Europe.

And think of the Spondylus shell, a spiny oyster from the warm Aegean or Black Seas. Its pearly, often reddish interior was fashioned into beads and pendants found in the burials of the first farmers spreading across central Europe (the LBK culture). These weren't local trinkets; they were exotic imports, jewels of the sea carried far inland, perhaps marking their wearers as individuals connected to distant places and powerful networks.

Beyond Simple Swaps: The Human Element

It's tempting to look at all this movement and just call it "barter" – a simple, tit-for-tat exchange. But that feels too clean, too modern. When we look at how exchange works in more recent small-scale societies, it's rarely just about swapping goods of equal value.

Think about gift-giving. As the anthropologist Marcel Mauss pointed out, giving a gift often isn't about the object itself, but about creating a relationship, an obligation, a bond between people or groups. That jadeite axe might have been part of a chain of gifts that solidified alliances, celebrated marriages, or settled disputes, accumulating history and meaning with each exchange.

Sharing within families or allied groups might distribute resources without any expectation of an immediate, direct return. And sometimes, materials might simply travel because people travel, following herds, visiting kin, attending gatherings, carrying useful or beautiful things with them. Those Palaeolithic shells? Maybe they were tokens exchanged when different bands met up for seasonal hunts, reinforcing shared identity. That ochre? Perhaps part of the toolkit for ceremonies that brought dispersed people together.

Reading Between the Lines

So, the archaeological record shouts loud and clear: materials moved, connections existed long before written history. But understanding the human stories behind that movement requires more than just mapping dots on a map. We need to blend the hard science of sourcing with the rich insights of anthropology, looking closely at where things are found (a grave? a workshop? a rubbish pit?), what they might have been used for (everyday tool? sacred object? ornament?), and why people might have valued them.

Labelling it all "barter" shrinks a potentially vast and vibrant world of social interaction – of gifts, debts, alliances, status, identity, and belief – down to a simple transaction. The real excitement lies in trying to glimpse that richer tapestry, decoding the complex human behaviours woven into the journeys of ancient stone, shell, and pigment. It's about chasing the echoes of conversations held millennia ago, spoken not in words, but through the things they cherished, carried, and shared.

Beyond Bread and Stone: The Social Heartbeat of Ancient Trade

Picture this: thousands of years before Amazon Prime, before even the jingle of coins in a marketplace, people were driven by an urge that went far beyond simple survival. They trekked across mountains, navigated treacherous waters, and crossed vast, empty plains, not just for a sharper flint knife or a warmer hide, but for... things. Beautiful things. Strange things. Things with no obvious practical use.

Think shimmering obsidian, sharp and glassy, sourced from volcanic hearts hundreds of miles away. Imagine the deep, celestial blue of lapis lazuli, wrested from remote Afghan peaks and finding its way to the deserts of Egypt. Consider delicate seashells, born in warm distant waters, adorning the deceased deep within continental Europe. Or the warm glow of Baltic amber, travelling south along pathways that became Europe's first 'highways' of connection.

Why? Why undertake such epic journeys for mere trinkets? The archaeological breadcrumbs – these out-of-place materials – tell a story not just of economics, but of the very fabric of early human society. It's a story about us.

Whispers of Power: The Language of Luxury

Long before logos and designer labels, possessing something rare, something difficult to obtain, something beautiful from over there, spoke volumes. It was a quiet broadcast of power, influence, and connection. Finding a cache of obsidian tools, far from the nearest volcano, concentrated in a larger settlement or a richer grave, isn't just geology – it's a hint of hierarchy. Someone, or some group, had the reach, the network, the pull to acquire these exotic goods. Like intricate Spondylus shell ornaments, painstakingly transported from the Aegean to Central Europe, these weren't just decorations; they were badges of honor, symbols worn by emerging leaders, a kind of prehistoric 'bling' that marked them out. The sheer effort involved was the message.

Threads of Connection: Weaving Communities Together

But it wasn't all about showing off. These precious items were the currency of connection. Think of them not as commodities, but as gifts. In a world without formal contracts, exchanging valuable, non-essential goods was how you built trust, forged alliances, and maintained peace. Marcel Mauss called it "The Gift," a system where exchange created social bonds, mutual debts, and obligations. Handing over a polished amber necklace wasn't just a transaction; it was weaving another thread into the social safety net, strengthening ties with neighbours, facilitating cooperation, sharing vital information, maybe even arranging marriages. Those "Amber Roads" weren't just trade routes; they were lifelines, corridors humming with human interaction, gossip, and shared futures.

Touching the Sacred: Objects of Ritual and Wonder

Many of these exotic materials resonated with something deeper, touching the realms of ritual and belief. Perhaps it was the colour – the celestial blue of lapis suggesting the heavens, the vibrant red of ochre evoking blood, life, or protection. Maybe it was the journey itself, imbuing the object with the mystique of its distant, unknown origins. Lapis wasn't just pretty; it adorned pharaohs' tombs and temple statues, linking earthly power with the divine. Red ochre, traded across continents since the Paleolithic, dusted the bones of the dead and brought cave walls to life, carrying a symbolic weight we can still feel today. These weren't just stones or shells; they were conduits to the sacred, pieces of the world imbued with meaning and power, essential for navigating the spiritual landscape.

Echoes Through Time: Stories in Shell and Stone

We see echoes of these dynamics in more recent history. Think of the Kula Ring in the Pacific, where shell necklaces and armbands constantly circled between islands. As Malinowski saw, these objects weren't used for anything practical, but their endless exchange, their accumulated histories and the prestige they carried, were the very glue holding the island societies together – defining status, alliances, and political relationships. Archaeologically, finding distinctive pottery styles or unique jade ornaments spread across vast regions of pre-Columbian America tells a similar story: webs of interaction built not on necessity, but on the shared value of symbolically charged objects.

The Enduring Power of the Symbolic

Ultimately, this ancient trade in the non-essential reveals a profound truth about humanity: we are meaning-making creatures. Value isn't inherent; we create it. Long before formal economies, people understood the power of objects to communicate status, build bridges between communities, and connect with the sacred. This long-distance exchange wasn't just about moving goods; it was a powerful social engine, shaping societies, fostering complexity, and proving that even in the deepest prehistory, life was about much more than just getting by. It was about connection, status, belief, and the enduring human fascination with the beautiful, the rare, and the meaningful – an ancient impulse that still drives us today, from diplomatic gift-giving to the global craving for things that tell a story.

Echoes in the Dust: Our Ancient Thirst for Connection

Long before screens flickered or coins changed hands, a different kind of connection hummed across the ancient world. Imagine the pull – the innate human curiosity to see beyond the next valley, the desire for something beautiful, useful, or sacred that wasn't found at home. This wasn't just trade; it was the earliest pulse of globalization, a complex dance of need, ingenuity, and social bonds, played out differently wherever people put down roots. Forget dusty textbooks; picture instead the landscapes themselves – the Fertile Crescent's river valleys, Europe's dense forests and high mountains, the vast and varied terrains of the Americas – each shaping unique highways of human interaction. By listening closely to the stories whispered by stones, shells, and metals, we can almost feel the pulse of these ancient networks.

The Fertile Crescent: Where Rivers Flowed and Obsidian Gleamed

Picture the world's first farmers, coaxing life from the rich soils of the Near East. Their world was changing rapidly, villages blossoming into towns. Here, exchange wasn't just practical; it was power. Think of obsidian, that volcanic glass, sharp enough to shave with, beautiful enough to covet. Imagine a piece quarried in the volcanic heartlands of Anatolia – perhaps near bustling Çatalhöyük – beginning its journey. It wasn't shipped in crates; it passed hand-to-hand, maybe as a gift cementing an alliance, maybe traded for precious grain, travelling hundreds of kilometers. Scientists using techniques like

Neutron Activation Analysis can pinpoint its origin, but it's the human story that fascinates: who carried it? What did owning such a piece signify? It wasn't just a tool; it was a status symbol, perhaps controlled by emerging leaders who understood the power of rarity. And it wasn't alone. Sticky bitumen from Mesopotamia, perfect for sealing boats or hafting tools, travelled widely. Shimmering marine shells, painstakingly collected from distant coasts like the Mediterranean or Red Sea, became treasured beads and pendants, adorning bodies and perhaps marking spiritual beliefs. In this land of concentrated riches – fertile soil here, volcanic glass there – connections became lifelines, managed through intricate webs of kinship, obligation, and nascent authority.

Europe: Mountains, Rivers, and the Sparkle of Ambition

Shift your gaze to prehistoric Europe, a continent of dramatic contrasts. Here, the story of exchange becomes a mosaic reflecting deep forests, winding rivers, imposing mountains, and beckoning coastlines. Imagine Neolithic and Chalcolithic communities (roughly 6,000-2,000 BCE) driven by the need for the best tools. Feel the grit and effort involved in mining razor-sharp flint from specific veins, like those at Grand Pressigny in France or Krzemionki in Poland. Picture blocks of this precious stone, carefully worked, travelling far overland or along river routes. Taste the vital tang of salt, painstakingly extracted from alpine springs like Hallstatt in Austria, a necessity carried across challenging mountain passes. Then, witness the transformative power of metal. The breathtaking gold artifacts found in the Varna cemetery in Bulgaria (around 4500 BCE) aren't just beautiful; they speak of incredible skill, accumulated wealth, and perhaps powerful chiefs who used these dazzling objects in rituals or diplomatic exchanges. Later, envision the spread of the "Bell Beaker" culture across Western Europe (around 2800-1800 BCE) –

not just distinctive pottery, but a package deal including copper daggers and archery gear. Was it migration? Shared ideas? Or perhaps mobile groups forging alliances, sharing technologies, and displaying their status across vast distances, connected by sea lanes carrying Baltic amber, river paths moving metals, and ancient tracks crossing the land? European exchange was a dynamic interplay between the land's offerings and the growing complexity of human societies, from tight-knit tribes to ambitious chiefdoms.

The Americas: Continent-Spanning Connections and Sacred Journeys

Across the vast Atlantic, the ancient peoples of the Americas forged their own unique networks, breathtaking in scale and purpose. In North America, imagine the Hopewell phenomenon (roughly 100 BCE – 500 CE), centered in the Ohio River Valley. It wasn't an empire, but an "interaction sphere" – a vibrant network drawing exotic materials to its heart. Picture obsidian flakes carried all the way from Wyoming, shimmering sheets of mica mined in the Appalachians, gleaming copper nuggets from the Great Lakes region, and lustrous marine shells journeying from the faraway Gulf Coast. These weren't everyday items; they converged in ceremonial centers, often buried with revered individuals in massive earthwork mounds. This speaks of grand gatherings, ritual exchanges, and alliances maintained through the giving of powerful, symbolic gifts connecting incredibly diverse cultures and environments. Further south, picture turquoise, mined in the arid lands of the American Southwest, making its way deep into Mesoamerica, prized for its sky-blue color. And in the Andes, imagine the perilous journey of the Spondylus shell, a spiky, vividly colored oyster harvested from warm Pacific waters off Ecuador. For Andean peoples, this shell held deep spiritual significance, linked to water, fertility, and ritual. It trekked high into the mountain chains, a sacred commodity connecting coast and highland. Millennia later, the Inca Empire, with its astonishing road network and state-run storehouses (qullqas), would build upon these ancient foundations, transforming localized exchange into a vast, centrally managed system uniquely adapted to the challenges of their vertical world.

Lessons Etched in Time: Why Ancient Connections Still Matter

Looking across these ancient worlds reveals timeless truths. The land itself – its mountains, rivers, coasts, and the resources hidden within – always set the stage, dictating what was rare, what was abundant, and the pathways people could take. But it was human society – our beliefs, our structures, our ambitions – that wrote the script for how exchange happened. Was it a gift shared between equals to strengthen bonds, like the Kula ring exchanges studied more recently in Melanesia? Or was it a flow of treasures controlled by elites to cement their power, displayed in grand burials or redistributed in state ceremonies? The scale shifted too, from neighbours swapping pottery to continent-spanning networks moving obsidian and shells.

These ancient echoes resonate powerfully today. Understanding how people exchanged value without money helps us grasp informal economies and gift-giving practices still thriving worldwide. The scientific tools honed to trace ancient obsidian or metal are the ancestors of modern techniques used to track conflict minerals or verify the authenticity of priceless artifacts. And perhaps most profoundly, seeing how ancient societies navigated resource scarcity, environmental challenges, and the fundamental need to connect offers deep perspective. It reminds us that our current, complex global economy is just one way humans have sought to reach out, share, and thrive together – a story written not just in stock tickers, but in the enduring human desire to weave threads of connection across time and space.

Whispers from the Dust: Sensing the Lost Economies of Our Ancestors

Imagine standing in the ruins of a forgotten village. Around you lie scattered stones, perhaps a few tough, fired clay fragments. Now, try to picture the life that pulsed here centuries, even millennia, ago. Can you hear the chatter of exchange, smell the cooking fires, feel the texture of woven blankets traded for sturdy tools, or grasp the weight of social debts paid through shared hunts? Probably not. What survives is like the faintest echo in an empty hall – the durable remnants of a world teeming with life, commerce, and connection, much of which simply vanished like breath on a cold day.

This is the archaeologist's great challenge and deeper quest: to listen for the silences. The story of the past is overwhelmingly written in stone and pottery because they stubbornly resist time's decay. The vibrant trade in food, the intricate beauty of baskets and wooden carvings, the warmth of furs, the essential knowledge passed down, the very fabric of daily favors and social bonds – these crucial elements often dissolved back into the earth, leaving barely a trace (Schiffer, 1987). We're left trying to reconstruct a dynamic ecosystem by looking only at the fossilized bones, potentially missing the warmth, the colour, the movement. It's easy to mistake the skeletal remains for the whole living creature.

The earth itself conspires in this vanishing act. Taphonomy – the science of what survives and why (Lyman, 1994) – tells us that the hard, inorganic stuff sticks around. This creates a kind of archaeological stage spotlight, brightly illuminating stone tool workshops or pottery kilns, while leaving vast areas of economic and social life in shadow (Rahman et al., 2021). Think of a grand feast, a cornerstone of community bonding and exchange in countless cultures. We might find the animal bones and maybe some serving bowls, but how do we measure the mountains of perishable food, the potent drinks, the vibrant decorations, the music, the stories, the alliances forged and strengthened around that shared meal (Dietler & Hayden, 2001)? How do we weigh the value of a healer's touch or a storyteller's knowledge, things that leave no artifact behind? Our traditional methods, focused on sorting and mapping durable objects, often fumble in the face of these vital "invisible" exchanges.

Worse, we risk dressing our ancestors in our own clothes. Applying modern ideas of markets, profit, and purely rational economic actors (the 'formalist' view) onto societies that may have operated under entirely different logics can blind us (Polanyi, 1957; Sahlins, 1972). For many past peoples, exchange wasn't just about acquiring goods; it was woven into the very fabric of kinship, ritual, and social duty (the 'substantivist' view). The connection sealed by a gift might have mattered far more than the gift itself. To ignore this possibility simply because social relationships don't fossilize is to tell only a fraction of the story.

But archaeologists are not just passive observers of dust and decay. We've become detectives of the ephemeral, developing ingenious ways to coax whispers from the silence:

Living Libraries (Ethnoarchaeology): We learn from contemporary and historical communities whose lives might echo the past. By observing how people today make, use, trade, and discard organic goods – how they weave social meaning into exchange – we build bridges of understanding to interpret the faint clues left by ancient peoples (David & Kramer, 2001). Binford's time with the Nunamiut, for example, showed how subtle patterns in discarded animal bones could reveal sophisticated hunting strategies and social sharing, knowledge utterly invisible in the bones alone (Binford, 1978).

Hands-On History (Experimental Archaeology): We get our hands dirty! By recreating ancient technologies – chipping stone tools, tanning hides, shaping dugout canoes, grinding grains – we learn about the skill, time, and labor invested, revealing the hidden significance of activities involving easily lost materials (e.g., Outram, 2008). It helps us feel the effort behind the artifacts.

The Science of the Unseen: Our labs become time machines:

Tool Tattoos (Use-wear analysis): Microscopic scars on tool edges tell tales of cutting meat, scraping hides, working wood, or slicing plants, pointing directly to the vanished organic world they engaged with (Keeley, 1980).

Chemical Ghosts (Residue analysis): Tiny traces of fats, oils, starches, or even specific traded goods like cacao, absorbed into pottery or clinging to tools, offer direct proof of forgotten foods and drinks, revealing ancient tastes and trade routes (Evershed et al., 2008).

Journeys Written in Bone (Isotopic analysis): The chemical signatures locked within human and animal bones reveal diets and geographic origins, mapping out food trade networks and the movement of people carrying goods and ideas (Price et al., 2002).

Understanding the Vanishing Act (Taphonomic Studies): By studying how things decay in different environments, we learn to predict what should have been there and critically assess how much of the original picture we're truly seeing (Lyman, 1994).

Thinking Beyond Things (Theoretical Frameworks): We employ concepts like Practice Theory or Agency Theory to focus on people's choices, habits, and social negotiations – the human actions that shaped economies, even when they left few durable traces (Dobres & Robb, 2000). We map potential connections even where the physical links are missing.

Think of the vast prehistoric salt trade across Europe. Salt itself dissolves, vanishing almost completely. Yet, we reconstruct these vital networks by finding specialized mining sites (like Hallstatt), unique pottery fragments thought to be salt containers ("briquetage"), and the sheer distance these clues traveled (Harding, 2000). Or consider a site like Çatalhöyük in Turkey. Understanding its complex life involves more than just tracing the obsidian tools from distant sources; it requires weaving together evidence from plant seeds, animal bones, chemical residues, building layouts, and burials to glimpse the intricate dance of farming, crafting, ritual, and exchange – a dance where perishable goods played a leading role (Hodder, 2006).

Ultimately, deciphering the economies of the past means embracing the absences. It demands humility about what we don't see, creativity in our methods, empathy gleaned from living cultures, and theories that acknowledge the richness of human motivations beyond mere objects. It's about learning to read between the lines of time, listening intently for the ghostly echoes of lives lived and connections made, long after the tangible proof has turned to dust. It's about giving voice to the silences.

The Social Soul of Exchange: Gift Economies, Debt, and Reciprocity

The Unspoken Promise: Why Giving is More Than Just Giving

Forget spreadsheets and bottom lines for a moment. Imagine a different kind of currency, one woven not from gold, but from connection, obligation, and the very pulse of community. This is the realm of the gift economy, a way humans have exchanged and related long before the first market stall ever opened. It's less about what you get right now, and more about the intricate social dance you're participating in.

Think of it like an invisible energy flowing between people. Marcel Mauss, a wise explorer of these human currents, saw this back in 1925. In his groundbreaking work, The Gift, he asked: why does a freely given gift feel so... binding? He found a hidden structure, a kind of social choreography with three core steps: you must give, you must receive graciously, and eventually, you must give back, often even more generously. To refuse any step isn't just rude; it's like cutting a thread in the social safety net. It can cost you respect, trust, and your place within the group. This isn't just about swapping items; Mauss realized it was a "total" affair, mixing economics with religion, law, art, and sheer social performance. Imagine entire communities caught up in this flow, exchanging not just objects, but feasts, songs, protection, even promises and alliances – a far cry from the quick, impersonal swap of barter where the relationship often ends the moment the goods change hands. Gift economies, Mauss showed us, are about building relationships that last, creating debts that aren't burdens, but bonds.

Voyages for shells, Feasts for Honor: Gifts in Action

Picture the South Pacific seas. Bronisław Malinowski, living among the Trobriand Islanders, brought us the stunning tale of the Kula Ring. Imagine men embarking on daring canoe journeys across hundreds of miles, not for food or tools, but to exchange specific, treasured shell necklaces (soulava, moving clockwise) and armbands (mwali, moving counter-clockwise) in a vast, ceremonial loop connecting dozens of islands. These weren't just pretty trinkets; they were heavy with history, carrying the stories and prestige of everyone who had ever possessed them. Participating wasn't about getting rich in goods, but rich in status, forging vital friendships and political ties. Under the protective umbrella of these Kula partnerships, practical trade (gimwali) could then happen safely. The Kula was the social glue, the trust-builder, across a vast archipelago.

And then there's the Potlatch, the legendary practice of Indigenous chiefs on North America's Pacific Northwest Coast. Imagine immense gatherings where leaders would shower their communities, and even rival chiefs, with staggering amounts of wealth – blankets piled high, shimmering copper shields, endless food. Sometimes, to truly display their greatness and untouchable status, they would dramatically destroy these valuable items. To Western eyes focused on accumulation, this looked like madness! But it was anything but. The Potlatch was a powerful engine of politics and social order – a way to publicly declare rank, validate inheritances, cement alliances, and redistribute resources through breathtaking acts of generosity (or destruction). It proved that sometimes, social standing – the ultimate "wealth" – was earned by giving, not hoarding. Some things, as Annette Weiner later highlighted, are so deeply tied to identity and history – "inalienable possessions" – that they resist being mere commodities, always retaining a piece of the giver's spirit.

The Echo of the Gift Today

Think this is all ancient history? Look closer. The spirit of the gift thrives in unexpected corners of our modern world:

The Digital Campfire: Ever use open-source software? Developers pour their skills into code, gifting it freely. Their "payment"? Reputation, community support, bug fixes from others – a digital Kula Ring of collaborative creation.

The Gift of Life: Donating blood or an organ isn't a transaction; it's often framed as a pure gift to society, driven by altruism and a hope that such generosity will be there for us if we ever need it. It relies on a quiet, communal promise.

Sharing the Spark: Academics publish research, gifting knowledge to the world, hoping for recognition (citations) and that others will share their discoveries in turn, pushing the boundaries of understanding together.

The Kitchen Table Economy: Think about your own family and close friends. Favors, meals, support – it's rarely tracked dollar-for-dollar. There's an expectation of give-and-take over time, but keeping strict score would poison the relationship itself. The bond is the point.

Ultimately, the enduring dance of giving reminds us that exchange is fundamentally human. It's not always about profit or calculation. As Mauss and Malinowski first showed us on shores near and far, it's often about the deeply felt need to connect, to belong, to build trust, and to weave ourselves into the vibrant, complex, and ever-moving tapestry of society through the simple, yet profound, acts of giving, receiving, and returning.

Forget the Flintstones Swap Meet: Was Economics Born from an IOU?

What picture pops into your head when you think about the dawn of economics? Probably two cavemen grunting and swapping a sharp rock for a furry pelt, right? That classic image of barter – the immediate, impersonal trade – feels like the bedrock of how we got started. But what if that picture is mostly a myth, a convenient story we tell ourselves?

Anthropologist David Graeber certainly thought so. In his game-changing book, Debt: The First 5,000 Years, he didn't just nudge that old barter story; he practically threw it off a cliff. He painted a radically different, and maybe more deeply human, picture of our economic beginnings. Forget the instant swap, Graeber suggested. Imagine instead a world woven together by a complex tapestry of promises, of favors remembered, of social "tabs" kept open within the community. He argued that intricate webs of credit, trust, and informal IOUs were likely running the show long before anyone thought of haggling over exact equivalents or flipping a coin. It wasn't about "what can I get right now," but about the enduring pulse of relationships, mutual support, and the quiet understanding of "I owe you one."

Whispers from the Past: Listening to Cultures and Clay

Where did Graeber get this seemingly radical idea? He listened to the whispers from different corners of human experience.

Living Libraries: Anthropologists, for over a century, have documented societies running on entirely different software. Think about the idea of the gift, explored by Marcel Mauss way back in 1925. Giving something wasn't about ending a transaction; it was often about starting or strengthening one. It created a gentle obligation, a social thread connecting giver and receiver, expecting a return down the line, knitting the community closer. It's the ultimate "pay it forward," built into the social fabric. Studies of groups like the !Kung San (thanks to researchers like Richard B. Lee) showed people sharing what they had based on need and the unspoken trust that help would flow back when fortunes shifted. Marshall Sahlins described vibrant "stone age" economies functioning on these ongoing relationships, not on spot-trades. Graeber pointed out that hard bargaining and barter often happened precisely where trust didn't exist – between strangers, or even potential enemies, not within the warmth of the village.

Dusty Ledgers: History chimes in, too. Journey back to ancient Mesopotamia, around 3500 BCE. This is way before the first coins jingled in pockets (around 600 BCE in Lydia). What archaeologists found weren't marketplaces full of bartering folks, but massive archives of clay tablets. And what were these tablets recording? Not "one goat for ten bushels," but debts. Meticulously tracked loans (often in measures of grain or silver, used like accounting units, not necessarily physical cash), rations handed out, obligations owed to the temple or the big boss. These weren't primitive scribbles; they were sophisticated accounting systems managing a complex flow of goods and labor based entirely on credit, promises, and who owed what to whom (Denise Schmandt-Besserat's work shows how early tokens tracked just these kinds of obligations). Imagine detailed records of farm loans, complete with interest, tracked over years!

Not So Fast? The Healthy Debate

Now, Graeber's idea, while compelling, hasn't completely rewritten every textbook overnight. Some historians and fellow anthropologists push back. Did he maybe paint barter as too insignificant? Is defining every social obligation, every favor, as "debt" stretching the word too thin? Critics (like historian Niall Ferguson, among others) suggest the reality was likely messier, with different systems – debt, gifting, and barter – bubbling alongside each other, depending on the context. Evidence for barter does exist, especially when different groups bumped into each other. Maybe it wasn't a neat, straight line from debt to barter to money everywhere.

The Ghost in the Machine: Ancient IOUs Today

But even with these debates, Graeber fundamentally shifted our gaze. He forced us to see the human relationships humming beneath the economic machinery. And the echoes of those ancient systems of trust and social credit? They're surprisingly loud today.

Think about ROSCAs (Rotating Savings and Credit Associations) thriving across the globe. Friends or neighbours pool money regularly, and each member gets a turn taking the whole pot. It's a bank run entirely on trust and social pressure – pure community credit.

Consider the informal lending circles that spring up in immigrant communities, helping each other get started far from formal banking systems.

Zoom right into your own life: "Can you help me move Saturday? I'll grab pizza," or "I'll watch your cat if you water my plants next month." That's it! That's delayed reciprocity, social credit in action, strengthening bonds through mutual obligation.

Even modern microfinance often succeeds by tapping into that pre-existing social glue, using community reputation as collateral.

Beyond the Swap: The Social Heart of Economics

So, was it definitively debt, and only debt, that came first? The jury might still be deliberating on the exact sequence and universality. But the evidence Graeber gathered, from anthropological deep dives into gift economies to the hard data on ancient Mesopotamian ledgers, makes one thing incredibly clear: our economic lives have always been deeply social. Systems built on promises, trust, and remembering who helped whom were not just common; they were fundamental, sophisticated, and likely managing complex societies long before the clink of coins or the haggling of barter dominated the scene.

The simple tale of swapping flint for fur? It feels a bit thin now, doesn't it? Perhaps economics wasn't born in a cold, calculated exchange, but in the warm, complex, and sometimes messy web of human promises and mutual trust.

Beyond the Balance Sheet: When Giving is How We Belong

Forget stock tickers and profit margins for a moment. Imagine stepping into a world where the most valuable currency isn't cash, but connection. Picture a place where sharing a harvest isn't just about feeding mouths, but about weaving families tighter, appeasing ancient spirits, and keeping the very cosmos in tune. This isn't a fantasy; it's the lived reality in countless communities where life's exchanges flow through the veins of kinship and the rhythms of ritual, a truth the great economic thinker Karl Polanyi called being "embedded" in society.

Think of it less like a marketplace and more like a dance – a dance where every step, every shared gift, reinforces who you are and where you belong.

Your Family Tree: The Original Social Network

In many traditional societies, your address book for giving and receiving isn't chosen, it's inherited. Who are your parents? Who are your cousins? Who did you marry? These aren't just social details; they are the map that dictates the flow of everything from a shared meal to lifelong obligations. Picture a hunter returning, not calculating his profit, but knowing his success belongs to the group, especially his kin. Sharing isn't just charity; it's the lifeblood of the community, a system of "owing" and "being owed" that operates on trust and time, not cold calculation, as anthropologists like Marshall Sahlins observed. Hoarding isn't just frowned upon; it's a betrayal, risking a chilling isolation far worse than an empty belly.

And when families join through marriage? It's often the start of intricate exchanges – maybe beautifully crafted goods, livestock, or years of support – that look less like a transaction and more like two families weaving their futures together, creating alliances that echo down generations, as Claude Lévi-Strauss illuminated.

The Sacred Stage: Where Ritual Commands the Flow

Life's biggest moments and the turning of the seasons often demand more than just acknowledgement; they demand spectacular acts of exchange. These aren't optional parties; they are vital performances on the community's sacred stage.

The Kula Ring's Eternal Voyage: Imagine daring sailors, guided by stars and tradition, crossing treacherous waters in the Western Pacific, not for gold, but for shells. As Bronisław Malinowski showed us, the Trobriand Islanders exchanged intricate necklaces (circling one way) and armbands (circling the other) in the famous Kula Ring. These items held no 'use' value, yet they were priceless – vessels of history, status, and the lifelong bonds forged between partners across the waves. The Kula wasn't trade; it was relationship-building raised to an art form, wrapped in ceremony and danger.

The Potlatch's Radical Generosity: Journey to the Pacific Northwest Coast, where Franz Boas witnessed the incredible Potlatch. Here, leaders like the Kwakwaka'wakw didn't gain power by hoarding wealth, but by giving it away – sometimes staggering amounts of blankets, canoes, food, even prized copper plates – in grand feasts. Some goods were even dramatically destroyed! Far from madness, this was a powerful declaration: affirming names, rights, territories, and social standing. Your influence grew with the scale of your generosity, binding guests in a web of future obligation. These events weren't just social maneuvering; they were deeply spiritual, often marking life's key passages and validating one's place in the ancestral story.

Andean Whispers to the Earth: Travel high into the Andes, where, as Catherine Allen describes, life thrives on a constant dialogue with the living earth (Pachamama) and mountain spirits (apus). Here, exchange takes the form of meticulous offerings – "despachos" – carefully arranged bundles of coca leaves, llama fat, sweets, and symbols, given to maintain balance, ensure good harvests, and nurture community health. Even communal work isn't just labor; it's often ayni, a reciprocal flow of help, shared meals, and ritual acts that reaffirm connection to each other and to the sacred landscape.

More Than Goods: Weaving the Fabric of Reality

In these exchanges, the items themselves are often secondary to the act. What's truly being traded are respect, obligation, status, history, and belonging. Each gift given, each ritual performed, reinforces the social blueprint and affirms the community's understanding of the universe. It's like re-enacting the stories of the ancestors, keeping the world humming in harmony, as thinkers like Maurice Godelier explored. To refuse to participate, or to do so incorrectly, isn't just rude; it risks unraveling the delicate threads that hold society and the cosmos together, inviting misfortune.

Echoes in Our Modern World

Understanding this deep embedding of exchange isn't just an academic curiosity:

Helping Hands or Hurting Habits? Well-meaning development projects can falter, or even harm, if they impose purely market logic onto communities that run on kinship duties and ritual cycles. Pushing individual profit can accidentally dismantle the sharing networks that provide resilience in hard times.

Beyond the Business Card: Anyone working across cultures knows that sometimes, building relationships, sharing meals, or exchanging thoughtful gifts isn't just pleasantry; it's the essential groundwork for trust, echoing these older traditions of socially meaningful exchange.

The Ghost of the Gift: Even in our hyper-marketized lives, think about how we exchange gifts with family and friends, volunteer in our communities, or participate in online sharing economies. These acts operate outside pure profit motives, reminding us that the human need to connect and reciprocate runs deeper than dollars and cents.

Ultimately, looking at societies where economy is inseparable from culture reveals a profound truth: the drive for profit is only one story humans tell about value. The quest for connection, meaning, belonging, and harmony with the universe can be far more powerful forces, shaping how we share, trade, and ultimately, live together. It shows us that "the economy" is never just the economy – it's always, inescapably, human.

Beyond the Barter Myth: Finding Real Exchange in the Spaces Between

Let's be honest, the old textbook picture of early humans swapping flint for furs in some neat, predictable "Age of Barter"? It's a bit dusty. Anthropologists, like the legendary Marcel Mauss with his groundbreaking work "The Gift," pulled back the curtain decades ago. They showed us that in many traditional, close-knit societies, life wasn't really about immediate tit-for-tat trades. Instead, it flowed through intricate webs of giving, receiving, and owing – exchanges wrapped up in relationships, status, and the steady rhythm of community obligation. Pure, cold barter, the simple swap with no strings attached, seemed almost... rude. Maybe even a convenient fiction, dreamed up by economists like Adam Smith trying to imagine a neat starting line for commerce.

But here's where it gets interesting. Just because barter wasn't the main engine driving village life doesn't mean it vanished entirely. Think of it less as a foundation and more as a clever tool, pulled out precisely when the usual social safety nets – trust, shared history, mutual obligation – wore thin. Barter, it turns out, thrives on the edges, in the fascinating spaces between settled communities and established relationships.

Picture this: two groups who barely know each other, maybe even view each other with suspicion, meet at a designated trading spot. Within their own villages, sharing and long-term give-and-take might be the norm. But here, with strangers? Trust is scarce. The guarantee of a future return is shaky. What do you do? You barter. You haggle, you inspect, you ensure the value is right here, right now. It's a clean transaction, a way to get what you need – that specific salt, those unique tools, the rare ceremonial feathers – without getting tangled in messy future obligations. Sometimes, as anthropologists like Humphrey and Hugh-Jones observed, barter isn't about building bridges; it's about making a fair exchange and then comfortably walking away, accounts settled. It's practical, efficient, and safe when dealing with the unknown.

We see this flicker of direct exchange in other liminal spaces, too. Think of those bustling crossroads markets that pop up in some traditional societies – places where different tribes or social groups converge. These aren't quite the anonymous, money-driven markets we know today, but they're distinct from the intimate sharing within a single clan. Here, amidst the noise and bustle, people might haggle directly, swapping goods for goods, especially if cash is rare or certain items just lend themselves better to direct trade. It's a different kind of interaction, more focused on the stuff and less on the long-term social dance.

And what about when relations are truly frosty? Consider the almost mythical "silent trade." Though debated by historians, the image is powerful: one group leaves goods at a spot, retreats, and the other approaches, takes the goods, and leaves their offering in return. No words, no eye contact, perhaps not even seeing each other. It's barter stripped bare, a mechanism for exchange across deep divides where even meeting face-to-face is too risky. It highlights barter's raw function: a way to move resources even when social connection is impossible or undesirable.

This knack for popping up at the margins isn't just ancient history. Look around:

When Crisis Hits: After a hurricane knocks out power and ATMs, or an economy tanks, what happens? Neighbours start trading skills – fixing a leaky roof for a bag of groceries. Strangers swap batteries for bottled water. Formal money fails, but the human need to exchange finds a way, falling back on direct barter at the frayed edges of the system.

Borderland Deals: In remote areas where crossing a national border is tricky or expensive, locals often develop their own informal barter systems. Farmers on one side might trade produce for manufactured goods from the other, bypassing complex regulations and currency issues. They are 'strangers' in the national sense, making direct swaps work where formal systems don't reach.

Digital Swapping: Jump online, and you'll find platforms where people trade clothes, books, furniture, or skills without a cent changing hands. It's technologically slick, but the core impulse is ancient: two people, often strangers connected only by the platform, negotiating the value of their items directly. "Is your unwanted sweater worth my spare lamp?" It's barter for the modern age.

So, the anthropological critique was right: barter wasn't the universal starting point Smith imagined. It wasn't the warm heart of community economics – that was the realm of the gift, of reciprocity. But barter is the ultimate pragmatist. It's the adaptable survivor, the mode of exchange we turn to when trust is low, connections are thin, or formal systems break down.

Organizing Complexity: Barter and Administered Trade in Mesopotamia and the Indus Valley

The Great Houses: More Than Just Bricks and Prayer

Imagine stepping into Uruk or Ur thousands of years ago. The air thrums not just with chanted prayers or royal decrees, but with the buzz of stuff. Grain pouring into colossal temple storehouses like golden rivers, the clatter of looms from workshops echoing through palace courtyards, the lowing of herds managed by institutional shepherds. The temples and palaces weren't just imposing structures; they were the beating hearts, the sprawling 'super-households' (oikoi) of the city-state. Think of them less as sterile institutions and more as enormous, bustling family compounds responsible for feeding, clothing, and employing thousands.

Their pantry was the backbone of everything: barley, barley, and more barley. Harvested from vast tracts of land, meticulously recorded by scribes whose clay tablets were the hard drives of antiquity, this grain wasn't just food. It was salary, it was stored wealth, it was the currency of daily life, doled out in rations that kept the wheels turning [Evidence: Those giant granary ruins and endless lists of names receiving their share aren't just archaeological curiosities; they're proof of a system designed to sustain a whole society]. Under the Ur III kings, this collection became an art form – the bala system, a complex rotation where provinces sent their quotas, a logistical ballet choreographed by the central state [Fact: Managing these inflows across huge distances hints at minds grappling with challenges we'd recognize today in supply chain management].

The Hum of Industry: Threads of Power

But these great houses weren't just about farming. Step inside, and you'd find another world humming with activity: textile production. This wasn't your grandma's knitting circle; it was state-run industry on a staggering scale. Picture thousands of women, their lives interwoven with the institution, transforming mountains of wool (from equally enormous state-managed flocks!) into fabrics [Evidence: Detailed records from Lagash feel almost modern, listing weavers, wool quotas, textile types – a glimpse into highly organized labor]. These textiles weren't just for local tunics; they were vital trade goods, the soft power spun into tangible wealth.

Chasing Horizons: The Long Reach for Treasure

Mesopotamia was fertile but lacked the shiny, hard stuff: metals for tools and weapons, sturdy timber for building, glittering stones for the gods and kings. To get these, the great houses looked outward. They became patrons of adventure, sponsoring or directing merchant caravans (tamkarū) on perilous journeys [Research: Scholars like Larsen have peered into these relationships, seeing the complex dance between state power and merchant enterprise]. Imagine these traders heading towards the mountains of Anatolia or the distant Indus Valley, carrying Mesopotamian surplus, chasing whispers of copper, tin, and lapis lazuli.

The Big Question: Command or Commerce?

And here lies the fascinating puzzle that historians still wrestle with: Was this all just a giant, centrally planned operation? Did the palace and temple dictate every deal, simply acquiring goods to redistribute according to their grand plan, as Karl Polanyi famously argued? The ration system, the state backing of risky trade – it certainly looks like a world built on allocation, not haggling [Evidence: The sheer scale points to centralized control buffering society].

But hold on. Look closer at the dust motes dancing in the archives. You see silver, weighed out in standardized shekels, acting suspiciously like money. You see barley itself used as a common measure of value [Evidence: Law codes like Hammurabi's list prices and fines, suggesting widely accepted values]. You find countless private contracts for buying fields, selling houses, lending silver (at interest!) – signs of economic life buzzing outside the temple gates [Evidence: Old Babylonian contracts scream 'private enterprise'].

And then there are the rockstar merchants of Kültepe in Anatolia [Research: Their thousands of letters paint an astonishing picture]. These Old Assyrian traders, while linked to their home city, weren't just state couriers. They formed partnerships, calculated profit and loss, worried about market fluctuations for tin and textiles, extended credit, and sued each other! They were pioneers of profit, navigating risk and reward with remarkable sophistication, their clay tablets breathing the spirit of entrepreneurship across four millennia.

The Mesopotamian Mix: A Human Economy

So, the truth? It probably wasn't one thing or the other. Mesopotamia's economy was likely a dynamic, evolving blend. Picture a river delta: the main channels are the powerful temple and palace economies, directing the flow of staples and labour. But feeding into them and branching off are countless smaller streams and tributaries – private deals, market-like exchanges, merchants chasing opportunities [Synthesis: Modern scholars like Van De Mieroop favour this integrated view]. Central control and redistribution likely dominated basic survival goods and large projects, while trade and personal assets danced to a more market-driven rhythm. The balance shifted with time and place, a constant human negotiation between security and opportunity.

Echoes Across Time:

It's tempting to see these ancient patterns reflected today:

The State's Hand: Think of modern state-owned giants controlling oil or grain reserves. Mesopotamia shows the sheer power of centralization for mobilizing resources, but perhaps also hints at its potential rigidities compared to more agile market players.

Securing the Essentials: Their state-backed search for metals mirrors today's global scramble for rare earths or computer chips – a timeless drama of securing strategic resources.

The Eternal Blend: The ancient debate between redistribution and market echoes in every modern discussion about mixed economies. Mesopotamia demonstrates that even in highly centralized systems, the human instinct to trade, bargain, and build personal wealth finds a way, creating a complex, often messy, but ultimately human economic reality.

Mesopotamia wasn't just cradle of civilization; it was a laboratory for economic ideas, leaving us whispers on clay of a world both alien and startlingly familiar.

The Silent Handshake: How the Indus Valley Built Trust Without Coins

Imagine stepping back four millennia, not into a primitive world, but into the bustling, sophisticated heart of the Indus Valley Civilization. Sprawling cities like Mohenjo-Daro and Harappa teem with life, trade routes crisscross vast landscapes (modern Pakistan and northwest India), yet something's missing: the jingle of coins in a merchant's pouch. How did this incredibly organized society, stretching over a million square kilometers, manage the intricate dance of commerce, administration, and long-distance trade without the pocket change we take for granted?

The answer, researchers believe, lies hidden in plain sight, embedded in the very fabric of their world: a remarkable commitment to sameness. This wasn't money as we know it, stamped with kings or gods, but a kind of proto-monetary understanding, a shared language of objects and measures that built trust and greased the wheels of interaction across hundreds of miles. Think of it as the civilization's secret sauce, its invisible infrastructure for getting things done fairly.

Whispers in Stone: The Weights that Spoke Volumes

Picture a marketplace, maybe in Lothal, a hub buzzing with goods. Instead of endless haggling over shifting scales, there's the satisfying, solid heft of a small, cubed weight, often carved from beautiful, hard chert. Archaeologists have unearthed thousands of these little guys across the Indus region, and here's the magic: they are astonishingly alike. They follow a clever system, part binary, part decimal, clustering around a base unit of about 13.6 grams.

These weren't just stones; they were tiny ambassadors of trust. Whether you were trading grain, precious metals, or vibrant textiles, these standardized weights ensured everyone was on the same page. Imagine the disputes avoided, the transactions smoothed! This shared system, stretching from Harappa to Mohenjo-Daro and beyond, was a silent agreement etched in stone, reducing uncertainty and making trade less of a gamble and more of a reliable exchange. It was a universal handshake, understood by all.

Pocket-Sized Promises: The Enigmatic Seals

Then there are the famous Indus seals, those intricate little masterpieces, usually made of soapstone. Thousands have survived, each bearing exquisite animal carvings (unicorns, bulls, elephants!) and symbols from a script we still can't fully read. But their context shouts their purpose: these were tools of business and bureaucracy.

Found pressed into clay tags that likely sealed bundles of goods, these seals probably acted like a combination of a modern corporate logo, a certificate of authenticity, and a shipping label. "This bundle is from me," it might declare, "and the contents are guaranteed." Imagine a package arriving in distant Mesopotamia (yes, they've found Indus seals that far!) – the unbroken seal impression would be a sigh of relief, a guarantee of quality or quantity from a merchant you might never meet. Their standardized production across the Indus realm meant these weren't just random carvings; they were recognized symbols of authority and accountability, little passports for goods traversing the ancient world.

Building Blocks of Order: Even Bricks Agreed

This passion for consistency drilled right down to the foundations of their cities. Wander the ruins of an Indus metropolis, and you'll notice the bricks – baked, durable, and overwhelmingly conforming to a standard size ratio (roughly 1:2:4). Think about it: building massive, planned cities becomes vastly simpler when your core components are predictable. Calculating materials, organizing labor, even training builders across different regions – all streamlined by the humble, standardized brick. These weren't just building blocks; they were blocks building predictability, laying the literal groundwork for stable, integrated urban life. It was the rhythm of uniformity making grand construction projects feasible.

The Indus Legacy: An Ancient Blueprint for Modern Trust

So, the Indus people didn't need shiny metal discs to run a complex, interconnected society. They built their economic foundations on something perhaps more profound: shared understanding, solidified in stone, clay, and fired earth. Their system of standardization was a non-metallic, information-rich network that fostered trust, fairness, and efficiency across immense distances – a testament to their incredible organizational genius.

And believe it or not, the whispers of the Indus echo powerfully today:

Think of ISO standards ensuring your electronics charger fits or a shipping container travels smoothly across oceans – that's the ghost of those Indus weights ensuring global compatibility.

Scan a barcode or use a digital ID – that's the modern descendant of the Indus seal, verifying identity and guaranteeing authenticity in our complex supply chains.

Trust in international financial reporting standards (like GAAP or IFRS) allowing investors to compare companies globally? That mirrors how Indus standards built economic confidence without borders.

Even cutting-edge blockchain technology, creating decentralized, immutable ledgers for trustworthy transactions without a middleman, shares a conceptual ancestor with the shared, understood system of standards that let Indus merchants trade reliably without a central bank.

The Indus Valley teaches us a timeless lesson: sophisticated economies thrive on trust and predictability. While coins are one way to achieve this, the Indus people masterfully demonstrated that robust, agreed-upon standards – a symphony of uniformity – can weave the strong, invisible threads necessary to hold a complex civilization together. It's a 4,000-year-old blueprint for connection and cooperation that still resonates in our hyper-connected world.

Echoes Across the Waters: When Mesopotamia Met Meluhha

Picture this: thousands of years before coins jangled in pockets, two mighty civilizations, separated by daunting deserts and the vast expanse of the Arabian Sea, were already intimately connected. Mesopotamia, the land between the rivers, pulsed with burgeoning cities. Far to the east, nestled along the Indus River, thrived another complex society, known to the Mesopotamians by a name whispered in their texts: Meluhha. Their story isn't just about trade; it's about the dawn of intercontinental dialogue, a sophisticated dance of exchange conducted entirely through trust, agreed-upon values, and the tangible weight of goods.

Clay Confessions: Voices from the Dawn of History

Our most direct dispatches from this era are etched onto humble clay tablets, the hard drives of the ancient world. Imagine Mesopotamian scribes, stylus in hand, carefully pressing wedges into damp clay. Under the ambitious reign of Sargon of Akkad, a king forging one of the world's first empires around 2300 BCE, these records boast of ships braving the waves not just from nearby Dilmun (think Bahrain) and Magan (Oman's coast), but from distant Meluhha itself, tying up at the bustling quays of Akkad. These aren't vague rumours; they are official acknowledgements, state-level pronouncements of a known world stretching far beyond their immediate horizon. Later, the pious ruler Gudea of Lagash, dreaming of glorifying his gods, inscribed on temple cylinders how he sourced precious materials from afar – exotic timbers and, specifically, "translucent carnelian," travelling all the way from Meluhha to adorn sacred spaces. These clay whispers tell a tale of recognized lands, desired resources, and deliberate, perhaps even royally sponsored, interaction.

Footprints in the Dust: The Archaeologist's Trail

If the texts are the whispers, archaeology provides the tangible footprints. Imagine archaeologists like Sir Leonard Woolley, digging layer by painstaking layer through the sun-baked tells of Mesopotamian cities like Ur. What did they find? Not just local pottery, but startling outliers: distinctive square seals, intricately carved with the unique script and animal symbols (that famous unicorn!) of the Indus Valley, thousands of kilometers from home. Picture these seals pressed into goods or documents, a mark of ownership or authority recognized far afield. Alongside them emerged fiery, etched carnelian beads – a signature luxury item crafted by Indus artisans, their beauty captivating Mesopotamian elites. Crucially, archaeologists like Gregory Possehl identified carefully shaped cubical weights, conforming precisely to the Indus system, turning up in Mesopotamian digs. These weren't just random stones; they were the keys to the entire exchange, the physical manifestation of a shared understanding of value, allowing for complex barter – so much grain for so much copper, measured and agreed upon.

The trail leading back to the Indus is fainter, a tantalizing puzzle. Perhaps Mesopotamian cylinder seals found in Harappa, or specific bead styles hinting at foreign techniques analyzed by Shereen Ratnagar, are echoes of this exchange. Why the imbalance? Maybe Mesopotamian exports were the essentials of life – fragrant oils, bolts of wool, sacks of grain – consumed or decayed over millennia. Or perhaps the Indus, rich in unique luxuries, held the more captivating hand in this long-distance game.

A World of Wonders: The Bronze Age Cargo List

So, what treasures traversed these ancient sea lanes? Weaving together the texts and artifacts, we can glimpse the cargo:

From Meluhha's Shores: Mighty timbers (rosewood? teak?) essential for building palaces and ships in wood-scarce Mesopotamia; the fiery allure of carnelian beads, perhaps lapis lazuli traded onward from Afghanistan's mountains, gleaming agate; precious metals like gold and copper; maybe even startlingly exotic animals – peacocks flaunting their plumage, chattering monkeys adding novelty to Mesopotamian courts; smooth ivory carved from elephant tusks; lustrous pearls from the Gulf; and potentially, bales of fine cotton textiles, a ghost in the archaeological record.

Heading Eastward: Likely shiploads of Mesopotamian staples – life-sustaining grains, aromatic sesame oil, warm woolen fabrics, maybe skillfully crafted metal tools or decorative items – harder to track, but essential fuel for the Indus economy or desired luxuries in their own right.

The Engine of Exchange: Royal Missions or Merchant Grit?

Who powered this incredible network? It was likely a blend of ambition and enterprise:

The King's Command: The proud inscriptions of Sargon and Gudea suggest grand, state-sponsored expeditions, dispatched with specific shopping lists for temple treasuries or royal adornment. Imagine massive ships, commissioned by the palace, setting sail for Meluhha's riches.

The Merchant's Gamble: Alongside royal ventures, envision hardy merchants, perhaps individuals or collectives, pooling resources and courage to make the perilous journey. Did Meluhhan traders set up shop in Mesopotamian cities, leaving their seals and weights as evidence of their presence? Did the island of Dilmun act as a bustling mid-way bazaar, a neutral ground where deals were struck? This wasn't haphazard; the standardized weights prove a sophisticated system of barter, a silent language of value understood across cultures, knitting together this vast network without a single coin changing hands.

Why It Matters Now: Ancient Routes, Modern Resonance

Unraveling the Mesopotamia-Meluhha connection is like finding an early blueprint for globalization. It's a powerful reminder that vast, complex trade networks aren't a modern invention. These Bronze Age pioneers navigated immense distances, managed intricate logistics, and built systems of trust and value exchange that functioned beautifully without currency. They show us the enduring human drive to connect, to seek out the exotic, and to build prosperity through interaction. As archaeologists scan the seabed for ancient shipwrecks and scientists use isotopic analysis to pinpoint the precise origins of artifacts, the story only deepens, revealing the stunning sophistication and ambition of our ancestors who dared to reach across the world millennia ago.

The Pulse of Civilization: When Barley Was Bank and Silver Was Security

Imagine a world buzzing with energy, long before the jingle of coins filled anyone's pockets. Picture the sun-baked cities of Mesopotamia – Ur, Uruk, Babylon. Life explodes along the rivers: farmers wrestle abundance from the earth, artisans shape clay and metal, merchants plot journeys across vast distances. But how do you trade fairly? How does a potter swap her beautiful jars for the wool she needs, especially if the shepherd doesn't need pots right now?

This wasn't just an inconvenience; it was a bottleneck threatening to choke the very growth of these incredible societies. Direct barter, the endless game of "I'll give you three chickens for that axe, maybe?", was messy, frustrating, and wildly inefficient.

So, the Mesopotamians, practical and ingenious, didn't invent money as we know it. Instead, they elevated the essentials of their world – the very stuff of life and desire – into something more: common languages of value. Enter the humble barleycorn and the gleaming allure of silver.

Barley: The Grainy Heartbeat of the Economy

Think of barley not just as food, but as fuel. It was the calorie powering the workforce, the daily bread filling bellies from the grandest temple priest to the humblest canal digger. Everyone understood barley. Its value wasn't abstract; it was survival.

Echoes in Clay: Crack open the world of cuneiform tablets, and you find barley everywhere. 1 Not just lists, but the rhythm of daily life etched onto clay: the precise sila (think a generous litre cup) of grain promised to a worker for a month's hard labor (often around 60 sila – imagine budgeting that!), the rent for a farmer's field calculated in giant gur measures (picture 300 of those sila cups!), the loans made with the expectation of repayment in kind, plus a little extra. Scholars digging through millennia-old administrative records see the birth of spreadsheets, written in the language of grain. Archaeologists unearth the standardized clay beakers and vast granaries – tangible proof of this grain-based accounting.

Making Sense of Worth: This wasn't just about tracking rations. It was about comparison. Is a well-crafted chair "worth" more than a strong pair of sandals? Instead of endless haggling, both could be priced against barley. Maybe the chair is valued at 180 sila, the sandals at 60 sila. Suddenly, their relative worth is clear (one chair = three pairs of sandals), even if no actual barley changes hands in that particular deal. It brought a shared understanding, a calculable logic, to the bustling marketplace.

Silver: The Cool Gleam of Lasting Value

While barley measured the daily pulse, silver became the standard for things bigger, farther, and more permanent. Why? It didn't rot. It was compact – a small amount held significant value. It could travel easily, unlike mountains of grain. And it shone with a universal desirability. But crucially, it wasn't stamped into coins; its power lay in its weight.

Whispers in Law and Trade: Look at Hammurabi's famous Code. Justice itself is often measured in silver: fines for offenses, the value placed on a life, the worth of a bride's dowry – all meticulously defined in shekels (a chunk of silver around 8.3 grams, maybe the weight of three modern pennies) or the larger mina (60 shekels). Price lists found on tablets reveal a world quantified in silver: a sheep might cost a shekel or two; a slave, depending on their health and skills, could fetch 10 to 30. Merchants heading out on risky long-distance ventures dealt in silver. Its weight, verified by trusty balance scales and standardized stone weights (smooth, heavy pieces of hematite or diorite found by archaeologists), was the guarantee. Archaeologists have even found hoards of silver – not coins, but rings, coils, and chopped-up pieces (Hacksilber), ready to be weighed out for payment.

A Universal Translator: Silver's genius was its ability to compare apples and, well, palaces. How many sheep equal one plot of land? How much copper is equivalent to a fine linen robe? By assigning a silver weight value to each, Mesopotamians could navigate complex transactions involving vastly different goods and services.

Taming the Chaos of Barter

This dual system – barley for the everyday, silver for the significant – was Mesopotamia's brilliant hack to overcome barter's headaches:

No More Guesswork: Forget arguing if five pots equal one goat. Price both in sila of barley or shekels of silver, and suddenly, you have a clear comparison. Value became less subjective, more calculable.

Making Change: You can't easily pay half a sheep. But silver? You could weigh out precise fractions using those scales and weights. Barley, measured by volume, also offered practical divisibility for smaller amounts.

Remembering Promises: How do you reliably track debts in a barter world? It's a nightmare. But "You owe me 5 gur of barley" or "Payment due: 15 shekels of silver" – that could be inscribed on a clay tablet, creating a durable record. Loans could be made, tracked, and repaid, even with different goods, as long as their value matched the recorded debt according to the silver or barley standard.

Echoes Down the Millennia

Is this just ancient history? Look closer.

Think of global markets today: the price of oil (like Brent Crude) acts as a massive benchmark, influencing countless other costs, much like barley and silver set the tone in Mesopotamia.

Consider places where official money becomes unreliable due to hyperinflation: people often instinctively turn to more stable foreign currencies (like the US dollar) or even essential goods as a trusted way to measure value and store wealth – a faint echo of relying on silver and grain when other systems falter.

Most profoundly, the very core of accounting – using a standard unit (dollars, euros, yen) to measure, compare, and record all economic activity – owes its conceptual heritage to those Mesopotamian scribes meticulously tracking debts and assets in gur and shekels.

The Mesopotamians, living thousands of years ago, didn't just build cities and canals; they built the foundational idea of economic measurement. By harnessing the power of barley and silver, not as coins but as trusted standards of value, they brought order to complexity, fueled trade, managed vast resources, and etched the first lines of the economic rulebook we still follow today. Their ingenuity whispers to us from dusty tablets – a testament to the enduring human drive to create clarity and connection in a complex world.

Diverse Worlds, Diverse Exchanges: Barter Across Indigenous Cultures

North America: A Continent Woven Together by Need and Ingenuity

Imagine a vast North America, long before maps divided it with sharp lines. This wasn't an empty space, but a vibrant tapestry woven from countless ecologies. Towering forests met sweeping plains, arid deserts kissed fertile river valleys, and shimmering lakes dotted the landscape. This very richness, this incredible difference from one place to another, wasn't a barrier – it was the engine of connection. Communities didn't just live in their environments; they lived with them, understanding intimately what gifts the land offered, and what it withheld. And in that gap, in the "what we don't have," the seeds of exchange were sown. It wasn't just trade; it was life support, diplomacy, and the very pulse of the continent.

Think of the centuries-long dance between the Pueblo peoples of the Southwest and the nomadic groups of the Southern Plains. Picture the Pueblo farmers, masters of sunbaked lands, coaxing life – corn, beans, squash – from the earth, shaping clay into distinctive vessels, weaving cotton into cloth. Their world was one of patience, cultivation, and settled communities. Now, shift your gaze to the vast grasslands, home to thundering bison herds and the Plains peoples who moved with them. Their wealth wasn't rooted in the soil, but flowed from the bison – rich hides for warmth and shelter, nourishing meat, tools crafted from bone.

Archaeology lets us peek into their lives, uncovering tangible proof of their connection. Deep within Pueblo ruins like Pecos, remnants of the Plains appear: tools made of bison bone, fragments of sturdy hides. Travel hundreds of miles onto the Plains, and the story reverses: shards of Pueblo pottery, kernels of their precious corn, even glassy obsidian, painstakingly sourced from New Mexico mountains, turn up in temporary encampments. These weren't random finds. They speak of deliberate journeys, perhaps to bustling trade fairs buzzing with negotiation and reunion, where the bounty of the earth met the riches of the hunt. This exchange wasn't a luxury; it was a lifeline, smoothing out the harsh edges of scarcity, a shared insurance policy against lean times.

Journey northward to the Great Lakes, a world defined by water and forests. Here, a different treasure pulsed beneath the earth: copper. Near the shores of Lake Superior, Indigenous miners extracted this "red metal," working it with skill – not by fire, but by patient cold-hammering – into tools, gleaming ornaments, and items imbued with spiritual significance. This copper, unique to the region, became a coveted symbol, traveling incredible distances. Imagine it passing from hand to hand, down winding rivers and across forested trails, its warm gleam eventually catching the light as far away as the Gulf Coast or the Atlantic shores. It wasn't just metal changing hands; it was connection solidified, prestige shared. Alongside this copper flowed other currents of exchange: razor-sharp chert quarried from specific, valued locations; furs trapped in the deep northern woods; wild rice harvested from shimmering marshes; dried fish preserving the lake's bounty; and crops traded northward from farming communities. Archaeologists today, like detectives of the deep past, can analyze the unique chemical fingerprints of stone and metal, mapping these ancient highways of human interaction.

More Than Goods: The Human Bonds of Barter

But to think of this purely as economics is to miss the soul of it. In Indigenous North America, exchange was woven deeply into the social and political fabric. Forget currency; the language of trade was spoken through intricate systems of barter, generous gift-giving, and the powerful weight of reciprocity. Giving a gift wasn't just handing something over; it was creating a relationship, a mutual obligation, a thread of trust between individuals and entire communities.

Building a trade partnership was akin to building an alliance, forging peace. Often, these bonds were cemented through ceremony and kinship, blurring the lines between trade partners and family. Picture the Calumet ceremony: the sharing of breath through elaborately decorated pipes, often crafted from sacred pipestone carried hundreds of miles from its Minnesota quarry source. This ritual wasn't just about agreeing to peace; it was about transforming strangers into trusted partners, ensuring safe passage, and weaving a network of mutual respect across diverse cultures.

These routes, carved by foot and canoe, carried more than goods. They were conduits for news, ideas, shared beliefs, and even ways to untangle conflicts before they flared. The intricate symbols engraved on shell gorgets found across the vast Mississippian world whisper of shared cosmologies and elite connections facilitated by this constant flow. When your well-being depended partly on your neighbor's specialized goods or resources, peace wasn't just preferable; it was practical. Warfare could sever the vital arteries of exchange.

Echoes in the Present: Why These Ancient Networks Still Matter

Understanding this vibrant, interconnected past isn't just an academic exercise. It resonates powerfully today:

Listening to the Past: Archaeologists continue to follow the trails of obsidian flakes, copper fragments, and distinctive pottery shards. Each non-local artifact unearthed tells a story, helping us reconstruct not just economies, but the spheres of influence, the pathways of migration, and the spread of ideas that shaped the continent. Sites like Cahokia still yield secrets about the sheer scale of their ancient reach.

Justice and Sovereignty: The documented history of traditional territories, resource use, trade routes, and inter-nation agreements provides crucial grounding for contemporary Indigenous communities fighting for land rights, negotiating resource management, and upholding treaty obligations. Knowing where ancestors traded, hunted, fished, and gathered provides powerful evidence of enduring stewardship and inherent rights.

Rekindling Connections: Across North America, Indigenous communities are actively revitalizing the knowledge of these ancient networks. This isn't just about preserving history; it's about reclaiming cultural practices, reviving traditional craft techniques tied to trade goods, and even re-establishing ceremonial exchanges that foster inter-tribal relationships today, breathing new life into old pathways.

In essence, the story of pre-colonial North America is one of extraordinary connection. Driven by the diverse beauty of the land itself, Indigenous peoples built intricate networks that were simultaneously economic, social, and political. Far from isolated groups, they were participants in a dynamic continental system where exchange wasn't just about goods – it was about survival, alliance, diplomacy, shared understanding, and sustaining peace across a vast and vibrant world. The echoes of their journeys, their agreements, and their ingenuity continue to shape the present.

Imagine standing on an Andean mountainside. The air bites, thin and sharp. Below you, the world plunges – maybe towards a hazy, dry coast where the ocean meets the desert, or perhaps tumbling down into the humid, green embrace of the Amazon. Above, icy peaks scrape the sky. How do you build a life, a thriving society, when everything you need – the corn that fills your belly, the warm llama wool for your clothes, the sacred coca leaf for rituals, the fish from the sea – exists in completely different worlds stacked one atop the other?

You don't just conquer the land; you weave yourself into its vertical threads. This wasn't about drawing lines on a map to claim one big chunk. It was far more brilliant. Andean peoples, long before the famous Inca, perfected what the scholar John Murra called a "vertical archipelago." Think of it less like owning a country, and more like having strategically placed keys to unlock the riches of wildly different natural treasure chests, stacked vertically up the mountainside.

Picture your home village nestled in a temperate valley, perfect for potatoes and maize. But you need more. So, your community, your ayllu, doesn't just stay put. It sends out tendrils, human connections reaching like living bridges:

Downwards: Maybe cousins, families, pioneers from your village settle in warmer, lower valleys (the yungas) or even near the coast. They aren't lost relatives; they are your lifeline to vital goods – the stimulating chew of coca leaves, the spicy kick of chili peppers, soft cotton for weaving, vibrant fruits, and the salty tang of dried fish or precious seaweed carried inland. You see echoes of this today when archaeologists find shimmering coastal shells buried deep in highland tombs, or highland potsherds near ancient coastal fires – silent witnesses to this constant flow.

Upwards: Other community members venture into the high, cold grasslands, the puna. Here, amidst vast, windswept landscapes dotted with ancient stone corrals, they become masters of herding llamas and alpacas – your walking larders, wool suppliers, and four-legged taxis. They also learn to coax hardy tubers like oca from the chilly earth. Great storehouses (qullqas) stand testament to their success, strategically placed to gather the bounty from these different "islands" of production.

These outposts weren't just resource colonies; they were extensions of home, bound by kinship and shared identity. The Inca later took this intricate, existing system and scaled it up dramatically, using organized resettlements (mitmaqkuna) to cement their empire's reach, but the underlying genius was homegrown Andean wisdom.

The Heartbeat of the Andes: Giving and Receiving

Now, how did all this movement of people and goods actually work without sprawling marketplaces or coins jingling in pockets? While simple swapping (barter) definitely happened at local gatherings (qhatus), the real engine driving the Andean world was reciprocity. It was the social glue, the cultural heartbeat, the unspoken promise that held communities together.

Ayni: The Sacred Balance. Think of it as the neighborhood watch, the barn-raising, the community potluck all rolled into one, but deeper, more fundamental.

"Today for you, tomorrow for me." It was the intimate dance of helping and being helped between families. Did your neighbour help you plant your field before the rains came? You knew, deep in your bones, that you owed them the same fierce energy when their harvest was ready or their roof needed mending. It wasn't about keeping score; it was about mutual survival, trust, and knowing you were part of something bigger than yourself. This ancient practice still pulses in many Andean communities today, a living testament to its power.

Minka: Hands Together for the Common Good. Imagine the entire community turning out – not for individual gain, but to build or maintain something everyone needed. Think of the breathtaking agricultural terraces marching up impossible slopes, or the intricate irrigation canals channeling life-giving water across dry lands. These weren't built by lone workers; they were the result of minka, collective labor for the community's benefit, or perhaps for the local chief. You showed up, you worked together, and everyone benefited from the shared infrastructure, the common strength.

Mit'a: The Imperial Echo. The Inca, masters of organization, saw the power of minka and transformed it into a state-managed system: the mit'a. This was a rotational labor tax. For a set period, communities would send workers not just for local projects, but for the empire's grand designs – building the vast royal roads (the Qhapaq Ñan), raising monumental temples in Cusco, serving in the army, or farming state lands. While it was definitely a form of tribute, the Inca often provided the workers with food, essential chicha (corn beer), and tools – a kind of large-scale, if unequal, institutionalized reciprocity, echoing the age-old Andean way.

Living History, Enduring Wisdom

So, the pre-colonial Andes thrived not just on clever resource management across dizzying altitudes, but on a profound understanding of human connection and obligation. The vertical reach brought the diverse goods, but it was the powerful currents of ayni, minka, and later mit'a that circulated energy, labor, and resources throughout the system.

This isn't just dusty history. It's a living legacy.

Walk through rural Andean villages today, and you'll see development projects succeed when they resonate with the spirit of ayni and minka, mobilizing communities through shared effort rather than just wages.

Observe how some families still carefully manage small plots at different altitudes – a quiet echo of verticality ensuring diverse harvests against unpredictable weather.

Stand at Machu Picchu, and see it not just as majestic ruins, but perhaps as a royal estate brilliantly positioned to manage and benefit from multiple ecological zones, powered by reciprocal labor.

The vertical archipelago and reciprocity weren't just strategies; they were the Andean soul, a way of life born from a dramatic landscape, enabling incredible cultural achievements and leaving echoes that still shape life in the mountains today. It's a story of human ingenuity deeply intertwined with the sacred bonds of community.

Before the Maps Were Redrawn: Africa's Economic Heartbeat

Forget the tired, dusty image of a continent waiting – passively, simply – for outsiders to ignite its economic spark. Peel back that faded colonial veneer, and you find a reality pulsating with life, innovation, and intricate connection. Long before European ships dominated the coastlines, Africa was a continent humming with commerce, a vast and complex tapestry woven with threads of trade, ingenuity, and sophisticated exchange.

Imagine standing amidst the energy of Jenne-Jeno, nestled in the Inland Niger Delta, centuries before the common era. This wasn't some sleepy village; it was a thriving urban hub, born not of war (its lack of walls for so long speaks volumes) but of collaboration. Picture the scene: potters shaping clay, their hands telling ancient stories; blacksmiths coaxing iron into essential tools, the rhythmic clang echoing through the air; fishers bringing in the river's bounty. These weren't people just feeding themselves; they were specialists, masters of their craft, exchanging their skills and wares in bustling local markets. These weren't just places to trade goods; they were the social and political nerve centers, alive with debate, negotiation, and community, beating to a rhythm set by market days – a truly African urban dream realized long before Arab caravans arrived.

And oh, the journeys! Think of the continent not as fragmented lands, but as interconnected realms linked by invisible, yet powerful, arteries of trade. Picture the Sahara, not as an impassable void, but as a challenging sea of sand navigated by resilience and ambition. Listen to the whispers of Ibn Battuta, the legendary traveler, marveling at caravans stretching towards the horizon, carrying precious slabs of salt – so vital they built houses from it in places like Taghaza – southwards, destined to meet the glittering allure of gold flowing from the forests of Wangara. This legendary dance of salt and gold wasn't just trade; it fueled the magnificent empires of Ghana and Mali, empires built on African ingenuity and control over these vital flows.

Further south, buried treasures whisper similar tales. Unearth the exquisite bronze work of Igbo-Ukwu in Nigeria, dating back over a millennium. Alongside local masterpieces, discover delicate glass beads from the Near East, hinting at trade routes stretching further than perhaps even Ibn Battuta imagined. Look east, towards the Swahili Coast. See cities like Kilwa rise, not in isolation, but as cosmopolitan ports, their harbors filled with dhows carrying the wealth of the African interior – gold, ivory, precious woods, and tragically, enslaved people – to meet merchants from Arabia, Persia, India. Imagine the glint of Chinese porcelain fragments found in the soil, tangible proof of a world connected by the monsoon winds and the shared language of commerce across the vast Indian Ocean.

Who navigated these complex networks? Enter the Dyula of West Africa, and similar merchant groups across the continent. These weren't just traders; they were master strategists, linguists, diplomats of the deal. Imagine them establishing communities far from home, building bridges of trust across diverse cultures, managing intricate logistics, and even developing systems of credit – promises whispered across distances, as valuable as the goods themselves. They were the connective tissue, the human ingenuity that made these vast networks thrive.

And how did they trade? Forget the simplistic notion of only swapping goat for grain. While barter existed, sophisticated systems of money flourished, tailored to local needs and values. Picture the shimmer of cowrie shells, tiny oceanic treasures journeying thousands of miles from the Maldives to become a trusted currency deep within West Africa – durable, portable, hard to fake. Imagine salt, not just as a seasoning, but cut into standardized bars, a currency reflecting its life-giving necessity in the Sahel. Feel the texture of specific cloths, woven to precise standards, representing stored value and labor in Central Africa. See the gleam of iron hoes, the weight of copper crosses, or the careful measuring of gold dust with intricate scales – all functioning as recognized mediums of exchange, units of account, stores of value. These weren't primitive substitutes for coinage; they were intelligent, adaptive economic tools, "special-purpose monies" reflecting diverse African economic philosophies.

Why does this vibrant past echo today?

First, it fundamentally rewrites the narrative. It dismantles the colonial justification that Africa needed 'saving' or 'civilizing' economically. It restores agency and recognizes deep-rooted innovation.

Second, the ghosts of these ancient routes still linger. Modern highway projects often trace paths worn by centuries of caravans. Understanding historical economic hubs informs contemporary regional development.

Third, the resilience and adaptability shown in these indigenous markets and currency systems offer powerful blueprints for understanding the dynamic informal economies that remain the lifeblood for millions across Africa today.

Finally, this history is a source of inspiration. The idea of a connected, economically integrated Africa isn't a newfangled dream imposed from outside. It's a homecoming. Initiatives like the African Continental Free Trade Area (AfCFTA) tap into a powerful, continent-spanning legacy – the echo of Jenne-Jeno's markets, the ambition of the trans-Saharan caravans, the cosmopolitan spirit of Kilwa. It's about reigniting the ancient heartbeat of African commerce.

Beyond the Price Tag: The Human Heartbeat of Oceania's Ceremonial Treasures

Forget your spreadsheets, your stock tickers, your relentless quest for more. Step into a different current of thought, flowing through the islands of Oceania, where the most precious things aren't things you use, but things that connect. Imagine wealth measured not in dollars, but in the depth of relationships, the weight of history, and the shimmer of pure prestige. This isn't a fantasy; it's a reality beautifully illuminated by anthropologists like Bronisław Malinowski, who peered into the soul of societies that value story over stuff.

Picture this: the vast, shimmering turquoise of the Massim archipelago in Papua New Guinea. Here, men with saltwater etched into their skin would brave treacherous open-ocean voyages, their canoes mere specks against the horizon. Why? Not for gold, not for land, but for the chance to exchange... necklaces and armbands. Seems mad, right? But the Kula Ring wasn't about fashion. The clockwise journey of the fiery red soulava shell necklaces and the counter-clockwise path of the cool white mwali armbands were threads weaving a living map of alliances, trust, and respect across islands. To hold one of these objects, even for a short time, wasn't just possession; it was to touch a legend, to inherit a story, to broadcast your standing to the world. These weren't mere ornaments; they were conduits of social power, humming with magic, kinship, and political ambition. The risk, the effort – it was all fuel for the fire of human connection, proving that the journey and the relationship forged were the real treasures.

Travel further east, to the Micronesian islands of Yap, and the concept deepens, literally becoming monumental.

Imagine massive stone discs, some taller than a man, weighing several tons – the Rai stones. Carved from limestone found only on distant Palau, acquiring them meant facing down the fury of the sea and performing back-breaking labor. Yet, their value wasn't just in their imposing size. It pulsed with their history: the difficulty of their journey home, the names of those who perhaps perished bringing them, the lineage of their owners. These weren't coins you jingle in your pocket. Often, these "stone money" giants never moved again once placed in a village. Ownership changed hands – settling debts, sealing marriages, cementing political ties – but the stone remained, a silent, immovable testament to wealth. Its value lived not in its physical presence in someone's hut, but in the shared memory, the collective agreement, the story told and retold by the entire community. It was value sung into existence, anchored in oral tradition – a bank built of history, not just stone.

What do these far-flung islands teach us, cozy in our utility-obsessed world? They shout a fundamental truth: value is a human creation, often having little to do with practical function. These aren't quaint relics of a bygone era; they are sophisticated systems built on what the great thinker Marcel Mauss called "The Gift." The powerful, unspoken obligations to give, to receive, and crucially, to give back – this is the invisible engine driving these exchanges, the very lifeblood of society. It's a dance of reciprocity that binds people together more tightly than any contract. Even today, as cash economies weave their way into island life, the echoes of these symbolic exchanges persist, proving their deep cultural roots.

And maybe, just maybe, we see whispers of this ancient wisdom in our own lives, if we look closely enough:

Think of the carefully chosen gifts exchanged between world leaders – often useless trinkets in practical terms, yet heavy with the symbolic weight of goodwill and alliance, a modern echo of the Kula's partnership-building power.

Consider the allure of a luxury watch or handbag. Does it tell time or carry things that much better? No, but it broadcasts status, taste, and belonging – a resonance of the prestige carried by a famed Kula valuable or a Rai stone with a storied past.

Why does a simple canvas daubed with paint fetch millions? Because we imbue it with the artist's reputation, its history, its cultural soul – a value born of shared belief, much like the Yapese stones.

Even when corporations invest in charities or environmental projects (CSR), they're often seeking reputational shine, goodwill, a kind of "social capital" – acknowledging that value isn't only counted in profit margins.

The Kula shells and Rai stones aren't just ethnographic curiosities; they are luminous examples of humanity's genius for embedding meaning into the world. They remind us that economies have never been just about cold, hard cash or practical use. They are, and always have been, deeply, profoundly human – woven from stories, relationships, and the enduring quest for connection and recognition. They challenge us to ask: what do we truly value, and why?

The Art of the Swap: Valuation and Negotiation in Historical Barter

The Heartbeat of the Swap: Why Barter is More Than Just Stuff for Stuff

Forget spreadsheets and market values for a second. Barter? It starts deep inside, in that messy, human place where want bumps up against have. It's that feeling in your gut when you've got way too much corn ripening, the clock ticking, and your neighbour's sturdy axe catches your eye because yours just bit the dust. Right then, that axe isn't just wood and metal; it feels like salvation, worth more than ten sacks of corn to you. But tomorrow, if you stumble upon three forgotten axes in the shed? Suddenly, your neighbour's offering feels... well, less shiny. Our own needs paint the first, vibrant colours onto the value of anything.

But we don't trade in bubbles. The moment you think, "My corn for that axe!" you step into the town square, figuratively speaking. Suddenly, your personal craving collides with the village's collective memory. It's the echo of countless swaps before yours: "Remember when Jia traded her woven blankets? She always got three chickens apiece." "Old Man Hemlock wouldn't give up his knife sharpener for less than a full day's labour." These aren't laws, but they're heavy – the comfortable groove of how things are done. Try to trade one scrawny chicken for that prized axe? Eyebrows will raise. This shared history is like the worn path through the woods – easier to follow, saving everyone the headache of blazing a new trail for every single exchange.

Then, scarcity throws a wrench in the works – or maybe a diamond. When the rains fail and only you have stored water, suddenly that simple jug feels like liquid gold. The desperate thirst of your neighbours mirrors your own potential need, amplifying its worth across the whole community. It's not just your gut screaming; it's everyone's. Think of tales from cities under siege – a crust of bread becoming priceless, traded for jewels not because the bread changed, but because everything else did. Scarcity re-writes the rules, turning everyday items into kingly treasures based on raw, universal need.

Yet, even with the upper hand, there's a hidden governor: fairness. Or maybe, the feeling of fairness. Push someone too hard, demand their heirloom locket for that jug of water, and yeah, you might "win" today. But tomorrow? You'll be the one nobody trusts, the person everyone avoids when their luck turns. Barter isn't just about the stuff; it's about the threads connecting people. We instinctively know that a deal feeling wildly 'off,' even if logical on paper, leaves a bitter taste. It can break the unspoken pact that keeps a community strong. Sometimes, keeping that goodwill, that potential for future help, feels subjectively more valuable than squeezing every last drop out of a single trade. It's playing the long game.

So, when two people finally shake hands on a swap, what's that agreed "price"? It's not just your desire or the village's usual rate. It's a unique alchemy, cooked up right there, right then. It's a blend of your specific hunger, their particular surplus, the ghost of past trades, the pinch of current need, and a healthy dose of 'does this feel right?'. The real magic happens in that back-and-forth, the haggling, the shared understanding – creating a value that belongs only to that moment, that place, and those two humans figuring it out. Even fancy online barter sites try to pin it down with points and credits, but we still haggle, weigh the feel of the exchange, proving that the messy, beautiful dance of human need and social ties always finds a way to lead.

From Barter Blues to a Smarter Shuffle: Our Accidental Invention of Money

Picture this: You're an ancient farmer, your back aches, your grain bins are overflowing, but your best axe just split. You need a new one. Now, the headache begins. You've got to find someone who not only has a spare axe but also wants your grain – right now, in the right amount. It's like trying to find a specific needle in a giant, moving haystack. This "double coincidence of wants," as the economists call it (cheers, Mr. Jevons!), wasn't just annoying; it was a monumental drag on getting anything done. Time spent haggling and searching was time not spent farming, building, or, well, living. This daily frustration was the fertile ground where a truly revolutionary idea began to sprout, almost without anyone realizing it: using stuff as a go-between.

Humans, being the clever creatures we are when pushed, started noticing something. Some things weren't just useful; they were universally useful, or at least widely desired. Take salt. Forget fancy seasonings; this was life itself, preserving food, making things palatable. It was so fundamental that Roman soldiers were famously paid partly in it – 'salarium,' the root of our word 'salary'! (Thanks, Bloch!). In farming communities, like ancient Mesopotamia, grain was king. It fed everyone, you could store it (for a while), and crucially, you could measure it. Imagine ancient temple accountants, meticulously tracking clay tokens representing 'sila' (think litre-sized pots) of barley – early spreadsheets keeping tabs on the community's wealth (Nissen, Damerow, & Englund showed us the receipts!). Those vast storage sites and tally systems weren't just about food; they were the bedrock of an economy (Schmandt-Besserat's work on tokens is fascinating here).

But just being popular wasn't enough for something to become the go-to exchange item. It had to tick a few boxes:

Lasting Power: Fresh fish? Delicious, but terrible money. It had to be durable.

Easy to Carry: Lugging giant stones for every purchase? No thanks. Portability mattered.

Snip and Share: How do you pay for something small if your currency is a whole cow? Divisibility was key – being able to make change. Early tools, arrowheads, even standardized axe heads sometimes fit the bill (Davies reminds us). Woven textiles worked too – light, easy to cut or fold.

The real magic happened with standardization. Think of the Indus Valley people (around 4,000-5,000 years ago!) with their incredibly uniform little cubes of chert weights. Archaeologists find these across a huge area, all following the same system (Kenoyer points this out). Suddenly, everyone's on the same page. No more arguing if your lump of stuff is worth my lump of stuff. This built trust and massively smoothed out trade. And who were the champions of this? The travelling merchants, the intermediaries, who relied on these agreed-upon goods to connect communities and build complex networks (Graeber explored this deeply).

And oh, the variety! Depending on where you were, 'money' looked wildly different. In parts of Africa and Asia, for centuries, it was cowrie shells – those small, tough, almost identical shells, imported by the billions (seriously, Hogendorn & Johnson tracked this). They were hard to fake and easy to count. Head over to Mesoamerica, and the Aztecs and Mayans were using cacao beans! You could buy dinner with a handful or, reportedly, save up thousands for major purchases like a slave (Coe & Coe chronicle the delicious history). It proves money isn't some abstract thing; it grows organically from what a society values and has available.

Then came the game-changer: metals. Copper, bronze, silver, gold – these were the superstars. Why?

Super Durable: They basically last forever.
Pocket-Sized Value: A small amount could be worth a lot (high value-to-weight).
Infinitely Divisible: Melt them, chop them, weigh them. Perfect for any size transaction.
Uniform: Gold is gold, wherever you find it.

Archaeologists find hoards from the Bronze Age onwards filled with "hacksilver" – literally chopped-up bits of silver jewellery, ingots, anything silver – alongside scales and weights (Rahmstorf shows evidence across Bronze Age Europe). Vikings were doing this too; imagine the Cuerdale Hoard, a massive stash of hacked silver found in England. This practice of weighing out bits of precious metal (Kim notes its link to early coinage) was the direct runway leading to the invention of coins, where the stamp guaranteed the weight and purity.

Interestingly, as Carl Menger pointed out, nobody likely sat down and invented money in a boardroom. It was a spontaneous evolution. People, just trying to make their own lives easier by ditching the barter headache, naturally gravitated towards using the most 'sellable' goods as intermediaries. They were acting in self-interest, but collectively, they bootstrapped the concept of money into existence.

And guess what? The ghosts of commodity money still walk among us. Think about prison economies, where cigarettes or instant ramen become the de facto currency – they're desired, relatively standard, divisible, and portable within that closed system (Radford's classic P.O.W. camp study illustrates this perfectly). Or look at countries suffering hyperinflation; when faith in official money evaporates, people might revert to using stable foreign currency (like US dollars) or even fall back on barter and trading tangible goods.

It's an incredible story, really. The journey from swapping goods directly to using shells, beans, metal scraps, and eventually coins and digital bits is a testament to human ingenuity. It shows that money, at its heart, isn't just about wealth; it's a tool born from the need to connect, cooperate, and make life a little less complicated. It's a shared agreement, built on trust and the relentless human drive to find a better way to trade.

Beyond the Swap: Barter, Secrets, and the Power of Knowing

Imagine standing in a dusty marketplace, sun warm on your back. Before you, a neighbor holds a sturdy-looking fishing net; in your hands, you cradle a basket overflowing with this season's apples. It seems simple: a swap, fair and square. But beneath the surface, a silent negotiation is already underway, fueled not just by what you see, but by what you don't know about each other's offerings. This hidden landscape of knowledge – or the lack of it – is the real heart of barter.

Think of it as trading secrets as much as goods. Maybe your apples, while plentiful, came from the slightly worm-prone tree on the north side. Perhaps your neighbor knows their net has a weak spot, carefully mended but vulnerable under real strain. This imbalance, this "knowing edge," immediately tilts the scales. The person holding the secret holds the power, able to nudge the exchange just a little more in their favor. It's the oldest game of poker, played with livelihoods instead of chips.

This isn't just about minor flaws. What if one trader knows a drought is coming, making their stored grain suddenly precious? Or what if someone knows the brightly dyed cloth they offer will fade dramatically after the first wash? When one side has a clearer map of the future or a deeper understanding of their own product's hidden truths, the exchange can become less a partnership and more a quiet conquest. This shadow of uncertainty, the "ghost of the bad deal," can even scare people away from trading altogether if trust completely evaporates.

So, how do traders navigate this fog? They become detectives. Watch them: running hands over wood grain, checking the teeth and temperament of livestock, sniffing spices, holding textiles up to the light. It's a ritual of seeking truth, trying to uncover the story the goods themselves won't tell. But keen eyes aren't enough. Ears are just as crucial. Whispers in the market, chats with mutual friends about past deals – "Is Elias's pottery usually this solid? Did Amina's last trade work out well?" – this web of community knowledge acts like an informal credit check, building a picture of reliability (or lack thereof). Sometimes, just waiting, playing it cool, can force the other person's hand, revealing how badly they need your apples or how willing they are to sweeten the pot.

On the flip side, how do you convince someone you're the honest one, especially if you genuinely are? You build a reputation, brick by painstaking brick. Every fair trade, every reliable promise kept, becomes currency in the bank of trust. People remember. They talk. A good name becomes your most valuable asset, encouraging others to trade with you, knowing the risk is lower. This echoes how cooperation itself thrives – the promise of future interactions makes honesty today the smart play.

Sometimes, you need to go further, actively signaling your trustworthiness in ways that are hard for a trickster to fake. Think of it as putting your skin in the game. Letting someone thoroughly inspect your wares, offering a detailed history ("This axe head was forged by my father..."), or even promising to partially undo the trade if something goes wrong – these are costly signals. They shout confidence. Centuries ago, faced with watered wine or shoddy wool, communities formed guilds, essentially creating referees to guarantee quality and build trust on a larger scale.

And don't think this intricate dance is just a relic of the past. Wander through bustling informal markets in many parts of the world today, and you'll see reputation is everything. Look online, at barter sites trying to recreate that trust digitally with star ratings and photos – a noble effort, though digital masks can sometimes hide flaws even better than a physical poker face. Even in the polished world of corporate barter, where businesses swap millions in ad space for hotel rooms or excess inventory, specialized brokers and iron-clad contracts exist for one primary reason: to manage the exact same ancient challenge of unequal knowledge.

Ultimately, bartering is far more than a simple exchange. It's a deeply human drama blending shrewd observation, strategic silence, the careful cultivation of trust, and the raw power that comes from knowing just a little bit more than the person across from you. It's a testament to our ingenuity in navigating a world where value is subjective, and information is everything.

Before the Quiet Click of Coins: Wrestling with the 'How Much?'

Imagine the sheer headache. You've got a basket bursting with gleaming dates, your neighbor has a pile of freshly tanned hides. How do you trade fairly? Your basket looks bigger, but are his hides thicker? It's the original human negotiation dance – a mix of guesswork, suspicion, and maybe a little shouting. Before shiny metal discs stamped with emperors simplified things (and even alongside them!), societies grappled with a more fundamental puzzle: how do we agree on quantity and quality when dealing with the messy reality of grain, oil, cloth, and everything else that makes life possible? This wasn't just about commerce; it was about building trust, the invisible mortar holding communities and empires together.

Tiny Cubes of Trust: The Indus Valley's Silent Handshake

Picture this: across a civilization sprawling larger than ancient Egypt, touching lands we now call Pakistan and India, archaeologists keep finding these... cubes. Not rough stones, but meticulously crafted, almost jewel-like weights of chert, dating back over 4,000 years (c. 2600-1900 BCE). Found from the grand cities of Mohenjo-daro to Harappa, these aren't random. They follow a stunningly precise pattern (a clever mix of doubling and tens: 1, 2, 4, 8, 16, 32... up to a hefty 12,800 units). Think about that consistency across a million square kilometers! It whispers of a powerful agreement, a shared understanding that transcended local squabbles.

These little cubes, the basic unit weighing about what a small handful of modern coins might (around 13.63 grams), were revolutionary. They were silent referees in the bustling marketplace. Your grain, my grain – measured against these impartial witnesses, disputes dissolve. Taxes could be levied fairly, grand building projects supplied predictably. These weights weren't just tools; they were a common language spoken across diverse communities, paving the way for intricate trade networks. They were tiny engines of fairness, ensuring that a deal struck in one town held water hundreds of miles away.

Feeding an Empire: Rome's Rhythmic Measures

Now, leap forward to Rome. An empire that vast doesn't run on willpower alone; it runs on grain. Keeping the legions fed, keeping the citizens of Rome supplied (the famous annona) – this was a logistical nightmare demanding ruthless efficiency. Enter standardized measures. The modius (think a decent-sized bucket, roughly 8.7 liters) became the heartbeat of the grain trade. It wasn't just an abstract idea; archaeologists dig up calibrated measuring containers in the ruins of market squares, like at Rome's bustling port, Ostia Antica. You can almost hear the rhythmic scoop and pour, the sound of the empire's metabolism.

And it wasn't just dry goods. Wine and oil, the liquid lifeblood of the Mediterranean, often traveled in amphorae – those iconic clay jars. While not perfectly uniform, specific shapes and sizes (like the well-known Dressel forms, holding around 26 liters) became instantly recognizable. These weren't just containers; they were messages. A certain shape might signal wine from a particular region, its expected quality, its volume. Stamps baked into the clay could name the potter or the estate owner – an early form of branding, a whisper of accountability across the sea. Sure, rules were bent, and dodgy dealers existed, but these shared standards were the empire's logistical backbone. They made massive taxation possible, kept the supply chains flowing, cut down on endless haggling, and built vital trust for deals done between people who might never meet.

Beyond Bulk: Weaving Quality into the Fabric of Trade

But what about things you can't easily pour or weigh? Think textiles. While harder to pin down archaeologically, whispers in history suggest moves towards standardizing bolts of cloth – agreed-upon lengths and widths, emerging perhaps in medieval Europe. Imagine the relief for a merchant: knowing a "bolt" means a predictable amount simplifies everything from storage to pricing. Specific weave densities or dimensions could even become shorthand for quality, a recognized standard across different towns.

Even the simple act of marking a container, like those Roman amphora stamps, tackled the tricky problem of quality. It was a producer saying, "I made this," offering a hint of assurance, reducing the gamble for a buyer miles away. It's about shrinking the unknown, making the world a little more predictable, one jar, one bolt of cloth at a time.

The Echoes of Agreement: From Ancient Weights to Global Standards

Were these ancient systems foolproof? Of course not. Cheaters gonna cheat, local habits die hard, and enforcement across vast territories was always a struggle. But compared to nothing? They were revolutionary. They slashed the time wasted arguing, built bridges of trust between strangers, allowed governments to manage resources on an immense scale, and helped everyone understand if they were getting a fair price.

And here's the beautiful part: these ancient struggles and solutions are alive and well today. That little Indus Valley cube is the great-great-great-grandparent of the ISO standard defining the screw threads in your laptop. The Roman modius echoes in the liters you pump at the gas station. The amphora stamp finds its descendant in the nutrition label and the brand logo on your cereal box. The standardized shipping container that makes global trade possible? It's tackling the exact same problem the Romans faced with their jars, just on a planetary scale.

Every time we rely on a shared measurement, a defined quality standard, a universally understood unit, we're benefiting from millennia of human ingenuity focused on one simple, profound goal: how to agree, fairly and reliably, on "how much" and "how good." It's the invisible architecture of trust that underpins our complex world, built stone by meticulous stone, measure by careful measure, since the dawn of civilization.

Making Barter Work: Logistics, Trust, and Community Frameworks

Whispers on the Wind, Weight on the Back: When Goods Were All We Had

Imagine a world without the satisfying jingle of coin, a time felt deep in the bones, where life's necessities were swapped hand-to-hand. A basket of ripe figs for a sturdy clay pot. A sharp stone axe for a pile of cured hides. Simple, right? But hold that thought. Feel the weight of that axe, the heft of the grain needed for a week's bread, the fragility of a fish just pulled from the water. Suddenly, barter isn't just an exchange; it's a physical challenge, a constant wrestling match against two unseen tyrants: Distance and Decay.

The Tyranny of Miles:

Think of the land itself as the first hurdle. Mountains don't flatten themselves, rivers don't part like the sea. Moving anything heavy – building stones, timber for a home, a season's harvest – was a back-breaking saga. Forget straight lines on a map; ancient paths, like England's timeworn Sweet Track snaking through marshland, tell tales of compromise, of routes dictated by passable terrain, not by haste. Archaeologists unearth these struggles, showing us how people literally navigated around their problems.

Picture the farmer needing to trade his grain. It's not just loading a cart. It's the slow plod of oxen or donkeys (carrying maybe a couple of hundred pounds if you were lucky, a pittance compared to later ships). It's the food needed for those animals, the food for the humans guiding them. It's the constant, gnawing fear of a broken axle, a sudden storm, or worse, bandits lurking over the next rise. Every mile was paid for in sweat, resources, and frayed nerves. Even the legendary Silk Road wasn't a superhighway; it was a series of calculated risks, favouring routes with life-giving oases, ducking the worst of the deserts and peaks, a testament mapped by geographers showing survival trumped speed. And the risk wasn't abstract. Sunken ships like the Uluburun, a Bronze Age treasure chest spilling tons of copper, tin, and precious goods onto the seabed, are silent monuments to journeys cut short, fortunes lost to the unforgiving elements or misfortune – a stark reminder of the very real perils faced.

The Tyranny of Time's Rot:

If distance was a wall, decay was a relentless clock. Fresh food – the juicy fruit, the day's catch, the butchered meat – was life itself, but it held the seed of its own swift demise. Exchanging these gifts over more than a stone's throw was often impossible. Imagine the fisherman's race against the sun, the desperate need to trade his catch before it turned foul, a matter of hours or days. Spoilage wasn't just waste; it was hunger knocking at the door.

But desperation breeds brilliance. This constant battle spurred incredible leaps of human ingenuity. It wasn't magic; it was observation and experimentation. How do we cheat time? How do we hold onto abundance? The answers echo in the archaeological record, whispered by chemistry. Traces of salt clinging to ancient fish bones, residues of fermentation in Neolithic pots analyzed centuries later, the smoky tang hinted at in storage jars – these are the fingerprints of preservation. Salting, drying, smoking, fermenting – techniques born from necessity, allowing food to travel further, last longer. Humans learned to build defenses against decay: airtight pottery vessels became personal vaults against spoilage, while massive, ventilated granaries, like those unearthed in Mohenjo-daro or Rome's port of Ostia, stood as communal fortresses, guarding the vital grain supply against damp, pests, and the ravages of time.

Wrestling the Tyrants: Ingenuity Takes Hold

History shows us people didn't just endure these limits; they actively fought back, weaving together clever solutions. Why haul tons overland when a river offered a flowing highway? The Nile wasn't just water; it was Egypt's lifeline, effortlessly carrying colossal loads of grain and stone that would have crippled land-based efforts. Trade routes pulsed with life thanks to innovations like the caravanserai – fortified rest stops offering safety from thieves and the elements, transforming dangerous journeys into more organized, manageable expeditions, often powered by the ultimate desert vehicle: the camel.

Real People, Real Solutions:

Rome's Annona: Imagine the sheer scale! An entire system orchestrated by the state to conquer distance and decay, feeding a colossal city. Fleets of ships braving the Mediterranean, specialized ports bustling with activity, colossal granaries standing ready – all to channel a river of grain, primarily from fertile Egypt and North Africa, keeping it safe and sound until it reached Roman mouths. It's a stunning example of infrastructure and organization as weapons against physical limits.

Pacific Islanders' Genius: Picture canoes navigating vast, trackless oceans using only stars, currents, and ancestral knowledge. How did they trade across such immense watery distances? They couldn't easily haul tons of perishable yams. Instead, they practiced a different kind of brilliance: they transported potential. Live pigs and chickens ("preservation on the hoof"), cuttings of breadfruit and taro ("seeds of future feasts"). They carried life itself, carefully managing risk and adapting their exchange to the unique challenges of their island world, a dialogue between human need and the vast blue expanse.

The Echo Through Time:

These ancient struggles aren't just dusty history lessons. They carved the world we know, shaping where people settled, driving the invention of pottery, ships, and preservation techniques. They reveal a fundamental truth: getting things from A to B, and keeping them intact, isn't just logistics; it's the bedrock of any economy, any interaction. The immense effort poured into overcoming the sheer physicality of goods laid the groundwork for everything that followed.

And even today, in our world of instant communication and global shipping networks, the ghosts of distance and decay linger. We still battle to get fresh food across continents, to move resources efficiently, to store them safely. The tools are vastly more complex – refrigerated containers, satellite tracking, complex algorithms – but the core challenge, the fight against the physical constraints of our world, is a story as old as humanity itself. It's the enduring human dance of need, ingenuity, and the relentless effort to overcome the space between us.

The Unseen Handshake: Why Trust is the Real Currency

Forget the sterile image of commerce confined to boardrooms and bound by legalese. Picture instead the vibrant chaos of a street market, the low hum of a village exchange, the lightning-fast deals struck across continents – often, without a single signed paper in sight. How does the engine of trade roar to life in these spaces? It runs on a fuel far older and more potent than ink and stamps: Trust. It's the invisible handshake, the unspoken agreement, the bedrock belief that allows us to build economic bridges between strangers.

This isn't just warm sentiment; it's a powerful, intricate social technology. Think of reputation as your social skin. In close-knit communities, whether a medieval Mediterranean port or a modern online forum, your past actions cling to you. Information flows like water – a kindness remembered, a cheat whispered down the grapevine. As sociologist James Coleman saw, these networks make honesty a strategic advantage. Cheat the system, like the Maghribi traders who embezzled funds centuries ago, and you weren't just fined; you were exiled. The network, your economic lifeline, snapped shut. The price of betrayal wasn't just lost profit; it was social death. Today, we see digital echoes in the star ratings and reviews that shape our choices online – a global village built on virtual reputation.

Then there's the magic of the long game, what game theorists call the "shadow of the future." When you know you'll cross paths again tomorrow, today's deal changes. It's not just about this single transaction; it's about tending a relationship that promises future harvests. Stewart Macaulay peeled back the curtain on modern business decades ago, finding that even sophisticated firms often let contracts gather dust, preferring the flexible strength of understanding and the promise of continued partnership. Why burn a bridge you need to cross daily? Ask the village lender extending credit based not on collateral, but on years of shared history and the borrower's desperate need to maintain that lifeline for the future. The value isn't just in the loan; it's in the continuity.

Deeper still lies the pull of kin and community. As Mark Granovetter pointed out, our economic lives aren't separate islands; they're deeply "embedded" in the tangled web of our social connections. Shared blood, faith, or origin weaves a pre-existing fabric of obligation and understanding. Within these circles, watching each other is natural, norms are clearer, and stepping out of line carries a heavy social cost. Think of immigrant entrepreneurs, as Alejandro Portes studied, leveraging the tight bonds of their enclaves to pool resources, share vital information, and enforce deals with the quiet power of community expectation – a built-in support system that often fuels remarkable success.

And when trust does fray? The community itself becomes the judge and jury. Forget courtrooms; think of the power of gossip, the chilling effect of a cold shoulder, the finality of being ostracized. Robert Ellickson's Californian ranchers didn't sue over stray cows; they relied on the unwritten laws of neighborly conduct, enforced by the desire to simply belong. Consider the millions participating in Rotating Savings and Credit Associations (ROSCAs) worldwide. Defaulting doesn't trigger lawyers; it triggers social exclusion – a devastating blow in communities where mutual reliance is key. This quiet, collective enforcement underpins billions in grassroots finance.

Even history whispers this truth. Before mass literacy, a merchant's seal wasn't just branding; it was a personal guarantee, their reputation baked into wax. Witnesses weren't just observers; they were the community's memory, making a broken promise a public betrayal.

Look around, and you'll see this invisible architecture holding up vast swathes of our economy. See the diamond merchants sealing multi-million dollar deals with a handshake and "Mazel U'Bracha," knowing reputational ruin is a far more potent threat than any lawsuit. See the street vendor getting supplies on credit based purely on a long-standing relationship. See the farmer participating in a local lending circle built on mutual reliance.

The absence of a formal contract isn't a void; it's a space filled by human ingenuity. We've learned to build order and predictability not just with laws, but with the intricate, powerful, and deeply human mechanisms of reputation, relationship, shared identity, and collective oversight. The strongest bonds of commerce are often not written on paper, but woven into the very fabric of our social lives. Trust, in its many forms, remains the ultimate currency.

The Hidden Currency: How We Thrive When Money Dies

Imagine the familiar weight of coins vanishing from your pocket, the digital glow of accounts dimming, the whole intricate system of official money sputtering to a halt. Panic? Maybe for a moment. But then, something older, deeper, and profoundly human kicks in: we look to each other. We begin the intricate dance of barter, trading what we have for what we need.

But let's be honest, trading your carefully husbanded firewood for a neighbor's repaired boots isn't like tapping a credit card. It's fraught with human tension. Can you trust this person? Is it a fair swap? What if they promise delivery tomorrow, and tomorrow never comes?

This is where the real currency emerges, not stamped with a president's face, but woven into the very fabric of our lives: our connections. Think of your family, your neighbors, the folks you worship with, the shared heritage that binds you – this isn't just fluff; it's social capital. As thinkers like James Coleman saw, these relationships aren't just comforting; they're potent economic engines, unlocking possibilities that formal systems can't touch. They are the invisible lubricant keeping the gears of exchange turning when the official oil runs dry.

The Village Grapevine: Your Original Search Engine

Forget Google. In a world running on barter, the "search engine" is the hum of community chatter. How do you find someone with surplus eggs who desperately needs their roof fixed? You listen. News travels over shared cups of tea, across fences, through whispers at the market stall. Who's known for their honesty? Whose promises are as flimsy as dry leaves? Who secretly has a knack for fixing radios? This intimate knowledge, nurtured through daily life, gossip, and shared stories (as anthropologists like Polly Wiessner observed in communities like the !Kung San), drastically cuts down the agonizing search for the right trading partner. Certain families or respected elders often become natural "brokers," not because they hold official titles, but because they sit at the crossroads of these information streams, instinctively knowing who needs what and who can be relied upon. You knew who to ask, and just as importantly, whose doorstep to avoid, all thanks to the power of the local network.

The Weight of a Name: Keeping Promises Without Police

What truly makes barter work isn't a contract enforced by courts, but the invisible hand of reputation. In a close-knit community, your name is everything. It's your credit score, your collateral, your bond. As Robert Putnam noted, dense networks mean everyone's watching, not out of malice, but because lives are intertwined. If you short-change someone, try to pass off shoddy goods, or fail to deliver on your end of a deal, word will get out.

The consequences aren't necessarily legal; they're social, and often far more cutting. It might start with a cool reception, being left out of shared tasks, or finding fewer people willing to trade with you. At its extreme, it can mean being shunned – a devastating fate when your survival and sense of self are tied to the group. This constant, low-level social surveillance, this fear of tarnishing your invaluable reputation (your social currency!), acts as a powerful force, ensuring most people play fair. Think of community savings clubs (ROSCAs) common worldwide; their success hinges almost entirely on this social collateral – the deep shame and exclusion that would follow if you let the group down.

The Comfort of the Known: Trading Fear for Familiarity

Let's face it, dealing with a complete stranger carries a heavy dose of "what if." Will they cheat me? Will they disappear? Are they who they seem? Embedding trade within a network of known faces melts away much of this risk. Trading with your cousin, your neighbor whose kids play with yours, or someone from your congregation feels fundamentally different. There's a shared history, mutual connections, an unspoken understanding of how things are done.

Kinship often carries potent obligations – you help family, and they help you. Shared identity, be it religious or ethnic, creates a kind of "moral neighborhood" where exploiting one another feels like a deeper betrayal (as scholars like Portes & Sensenbrenner explored). Studies show that within these enclaves, trust blossoms more readily, smoothing the path for economic activity, including the vital back-and-forth of informal exchange. You simply breathe easier trading with someone whose story you know, whose place in the community tapestry is clear.

Where It Plays Out Today:

This isn't just ancient history. Watch:

Immigrant Entrepreneurs: See how newcomers build thriving businesses, often leaning heavily on shared roots for loans (hello, ROSCAs!), reliable help, market insights, and loyal customers. Reputation is king.

After the Storm: When disaster strikes (like Hurricane Katrina), formal systems collapse. What emerges? Neighbors helping neighbors, churches organizing aid, pre-existing social ties becoming literal lifelines for sharing resources and rebuilding – a massive, urgent barter system powered by trust built over years. Stronger communities bounce back faster.

Local Exchange Systems (LETS): Even modern attempts to create cashless trading circles rely utterly on the same old magic: community trust, reputation, and shared accountability to make the "local dollars" flow.

So, when the official economy seems fragile, remember the resilient, ancient system humming beneath it. Social capital – that web of relationships, trust, and shared knowledge – isn't just a safety net; it's the very lifeblood that allows communities to sustain themselves, proving that our greatest wealth often lies not in our wallets, but in each other.

The Original Social Network: Trust Etched in Memory

Imagine a world knit tight, not by Wi-Fi, but by shared breath and mutual reliance. Long before ledgers or spreadsheets, the most vital accounting tool pulsed within each person: memory. Picture it – the warmth of a neighbor helping rebuild your storm-damaged roof, the shared bounty of a successful hunt, the handful of seeds borrowed in lean times. These weren't casual favors; they were threads woven into the very fabric of community life, logged in the intricate database of the human mind.

This was the era of the gift that binds. As thinkers like Marcel Mauss illuminated, giving wasn't just generosity; it was an investment, creating a subtle, powerful obligation to reciprocate. Your reputation wasn't just about being liked; it was your credit score, your social capital. Being known as someone who "made good" on their unspoken debts was paramount. Forget a formal contract – you had the wisdom of elders, respected figures whose memories served as living, breathing ledgers, vouching for agreements and recalling outstanding balances. Failing to honor these invisible debts wasn't merely impolite; in small, interdependent groups, it courted social frostbite, even exile – a potent consequence when the group was your world [Source: Graeber, D. (2011)]. But memory, powerful as it is, can fray, especially as communities grew, deals became more complex, or time stretched between the promise and its fulfillment. The human mind needed a helping hand.

Making Memory Tangible: Notches, Knots, and Handshakes in Wood

So, human cleverness turned to the physical world. Enter the humble tally stick. Simple, yet profound. A piece of wood or bone, carefully notched – each mark a silent testament to a quantity, a deal struck, a promise made. Think of the elegant genius of splitting the stick lengthwise: each party held half, the jagged edges fitting perfectly, creating an undeniable, tamper-proof record of the original agreement. It was a physical handshake frozen in time, a practice echoing from the mists of prehistory (like the ancient Lebombo bone, perhaps a 35,000-year-old counter [Source: Bogoshi, J., et al. (1987)]) right across continents and millennia [Source: Baxandall, M. (1971) - on later use]. Simple tools for profound concepts: trust and verification.

Then, imagine that concept blossoming into something far more intricate: the quipu of the Andes. Not just notches, but a cascade of knotted strings, a tactile language woven by the Inca and their predecessors. Different knots, colors, placements – a sophisticated system humming with information. While the full extent of their meaning remains debated (did they whisper stories, or just count llamas?), scholars like Gary Urton reveal their power to track tribute, census data, the rhythms of the calendar – a complex tapestry of state-level accounting woven without a single written word [Sources: Urton, G. (2003); Urton, G. & Brezine, C. J. (2005)]. It was data visualization you could hold in your hands, a quantum leap beyond simple tallies.

Freezing Promises: Seals, Symbols, and the Dawn of Writing

The real revolution, however, arrived with the power to freeze a promise onto clay. In the bustling cities of Mesopotamia, the cylinder seal emerged. More than just a pretty carving, rolling this personal stone across wet clay was like signing your name in triplicate – it authenticated documents, claimed ownership, sealed jars, making accountability visible and personal [Source: Collon, D. (2005)]. A sealed clay tag wasn't just a label; it was a mark of who was responsible.

Around the same time, perhaps evolving from simple clay tokens representing goods (a cone for grain, a sphere for an animal?), came the scratches and impressions that would bloom into cuneiform [Source: Schmandt-Besserat, D. (1996)]. And what were these earliest written records about? Not epic poems, but the nitty-gritty of life: lists of goods, ration distributions, and crucially, records of debt [Source: Nissen, H. J., et al. (1993)]. Writing offered an unambiguous, lasting, and scalable way to track the increasingly complex web of obligations in burgeoning temples, palaces, and cities. It was the birth certificate of bureaucracy, written in mud.

Ancient Echoes in Our Modern World

Think these old ways are just dust and museum pieces? Look closer.

That informal "susu" or ROSCA your grandmother participates in? Where trust and community pressure ensure everyone pays in and gets their payout? That's the spirit of ancient social vouching, alive today in communities worldwide [Source: Gugerty, M. K. (2007)].

The success of microfinance often relies less on collateral and more on group lending – neighbours implicitly guaranteeing each other's small loans. It's the power of the community ledger, reimagined [Source: Yunus, M. (2007)].

Even the cutting edge of blockchain – a distributed, verifiable, hard-to-alter ledger – carries a conceptual echo of that split tally stick. Both aim for a transparent, trustworthy record held by many, making cheating difficult.

From the fleeting memory within a tight-knit clan to the enduring symbols baked onto clay tablets, this journey isn't just about accounting. It's a profoundly human story about our relentless drive to build systems of trust, fairness, and cooperation across time and distance. These ancient innovations weren't just about counting sheep; they were about weaving the very fabric of complex society, a fabric we still rely on today.

Arteries of Exchange: Barter within the Silk Road's Monetary Pluralism

The Pulse of the Oasis: Where Worlds Met and Money Talked (in Many Tongues)

Picture this: Turfan. Not a museum exhibit, but a living, breathing town choked with dust kicked up by camels, donkeys, and a thousand sandaled feet. The air isn't just humming – it's a thick soup of smells: pungent spices from faraway lands, roasting meat, the sharp tang of animal dung, maybe even the faint, exotic perfume of sandalwood clinging to a merchant's robe. And the sound! A chaotic symphony of languages – guttural Sogdian haggling with clipped Han Chinese, the lilt of Persian poetry recited beside the drone of Buddhist chants, traders shouting prices, children laughing, coins clinking, silk rustling like secrets.

This wasn't an economy with neat rules you could learn from a textbook. It was a living, breathing organism, constantly adapting. Forget a single currency; think of value as a flowing river with many currents.

Deep down, at the most human level, there was the simple swap. "Your sturdy pot for my bag of dates?" This wasn't grand commerce recorded by scribes; it was the heartbeat of daily life, the unspoken agreements between neighbours, the quick deals struck in dusty alleyways when coins were scarce or simply not the point. It's the kind of exchange built on need, trust, and knowing the worth of a thing in your hands versus their hands, a wisdom older than any emperor's face on metal. You won't find many receipts for this, but you feel it in the foundations of the place.

But Turfan thrived on bigger things. And the biggest star, the one that gave these routes their name, was silk. Not just beautiful fabric, but money. Imagine unrolling a bolt – sunlight catching the shimmering threads. This wasn't just cloth; it was a standardized unit, measured, recognized, almost revered. Those fragile documents dug from the sand? They're not dry accounts; they're snapshots of life: a vineyard bought not with gold, but with the promise of dozens of rolls of this woven light. A farmer pays a fine, not with clinking metal, but with the very stuff emperors craved. Each bolt, perhaps 15 paces long, was a solid, tangible piece of wealth.

And then there was grain. Less glamorous, perhaps, but just as vital. This was the currency of survival, the gritty reality of the oasis. Wheat and millet measured out paid the labourers who dug the irrigation channels, filled the bellies of soldiers, and settled local tax debts. It was the steady, earthy bass note beneath the silk's high melody. You could eat your wages, solid proof of a day's work.

Of course, the emperors wanted their say. Their power rippled outwards in the form of coins. Imagine the satisfying heft of a Sasanian silver drachm, minted in Persia but trusted far into the East – the go-to for serious deals, its silver content a reliable promise. Hoards of these coins, unearthed centuries later, feel like buried pirate treasure, whispers of fortunes made and lost. From the other direction, the gleam of Byzantine gold solidi – maybe fewer in number, sometimes even pierced to be worn as a badge of wealth, but representing the long reach of Rome's successor, reserved for the highest stakes. And buzzing through the local markets, the everyday transactions, were the strings of Chinese bronze cash – the small change, the pocket money, familiar and essential for buying a bite to eat or a simple tool.

The real magic? It wasn't just having all these forms of value; it was the people who could dance between them. Picture the Sogdian merchant, eyes sharp, mind sharper, a human calculator fluent in silk bolts, silver weight, and grain measures. His promises, recorded in letters carried across treacherous mountains, dealt in complex webs of debt and partnership, implicitly translating one form of wealth into another. Contracts found in Turfan show this genius explicitly: "You owe me ten silver coins, but fine, pay me fifteen bolts of silk by next spring." This wasn't chaos; it was sophisticated adaptation. It required trust, complex mental arithmetic, and networks that spanned cultures and deserts.

Why does this ancient, messy system still fascinate us? Because it's a powerful story about human ingenuity. It shows us that economies aren't just abstract forces; they are built by people finding ways to connect, to trade, to survive and thrive, even when their rulers, languages, and ideas of 'money' are worlds apart. Look around today – at border towns juggling currencies, at online platforms mixing cash, crypto, and direct swaps – and you see echoes of that same Silk Road spirit. It's a timeless reminder that the need to exchange, to connect, to build something together, will always find a way, weaving a vibrant tapestry of commerce from whatever threads are available – be it barter, bolts of silk, or bits of code. The Silk Road wasn't just a path; it was a pulse, driven by the endlessly creative human drive to make a deal.

The Emperor's Nightmare and the Weaver's Thread: Geopolitics Spun from Silk and Steeds

Forget the romantic notion of the Silk Road as a simple highway for treasure-seeking merchants. Peel back that shimmering layer, and you find something far more primal, more urgent: a centuries-long heartbeat of strategic survival played out in bolts of luminous fabric and the thunder of warhorses. This wasn't just trade; it was the high-stakes diplomacy of empires, where the softest silk became the currency for the hardest power.

Imagine being a Han Dynasty emperor (206 BCE – 220 CE), staring northwards. The reports filtering back aren't of bustling markets, but of terrifying shadows on the horizon – the Xiongnu nomads, masters of the horse and bow. Sima Qian, writing not just history but the anxieties of his age in the Shiji, paints a chilling picture: Chinese foot soldiers, brave but slow, swallowed by whirlwind cavalry attacks that materialized from the steppes like ghosts. This wasn't a border skirmish; it was an existential dread. How do you fight the wind? How do you counter warriors who lived in the saddle?

The answer wasn't found in Chinese fields, but far to the west, in distant valleys like Ferghana. Whispers turned to legends of "heavenly horses" (tianma) – steeds possessing near-mythical endurance, speed, and strength. For emperors like the ambitious Wu of Han, these weren't just animals; they were the desperately needed equalizer, the key to survival. His obsession, chronicled in the Book of Han, wasn't about exploration for its own sake; it was a state-sponsored hunt for living weapons. Imagine the immense gamble: launching vast expeditions, bleeding the treasury dry, sacrificing thousands of soldiers not in battle, but on treacherous journeys just to secure a reliable supply of these four-legged engines of war. This wasn't commerce; it was a military imperative bordering on desperation.

And what could China offer in return? Its own unique treasure, a secret whispered across continents: silk. For centuries, the art of its creation was guarded jealousy, making it more valuable than gold in many lands. Picture the scene: Nomadic chieftains and Central Asian kings, rulers whose power stemmed from controlling vast grasslands and trade arteries, receiving emissaries bearing bolts of this incredible fabric. It was impossibly light, shimmered with captured light, and felt like nothing else on earth. For them, it wasn't just clothing; it was pure status, a symbol of power easily traded further west, a lubricant for their own political machines, as scholars like Thomas Barfield have shown.

But the Chinese state played this hand with cunning calculation. Silk wasn't simply sold; it was deployed. It flowed outwards as part of the intricate tribute system – sometimes as lavish gifts to soothe restless neighbors, sometimes as subsidies to buy temporary peace or forge alliances against a common foe. Offering silk specifically for horses became a masterstroke of foreign policy: acquire the shield while simultaneously managing the potential sword. The "price" wasn't set by supply and demand alone, but by the political temperature. In times of crisis, when the northern threat loomed large, the value of a single, prime warhorse could soar to dozens upon dozens of bolts of the finest silk – a testament to how fear can warp any market.

While lone merchants surely navigated the dusty trails, seeking their own fortunes, make no mistake: the core of this exchange pulsed with imperial direction. Frontier markets were often state-run, procurement overseen by officials, the military itself directly involved. This wasn't Adam Smith's invisible hand; it was the very visible, often forceful, hand of the state reaching out to secure a resource deemed essential for its very existence.

Echoes in Our Modern World:

Does this ancient dance of strategic barter sound strangely familiar? It should. The fundamental logic – leveraging a unique national strength to acquire a critical need, driven by security and geopolitical positioning – reverberates powerfully today:

Energy for Arms & Influence: Think of nations rich in oil or gas ("black gold") exchanging guaranteed energy supplies for cutting-edge military hardware, sophisticated technology, or massive infrastructure projects from industrial powers. Like silk for horses, it's rarely just about the money; it's about securing energy flows, gaining military edges, or cementing alliances on the global stage.

Market Keys for Tech Secrets: Imagine a rapidly developing nation granting a global tech giant privileged access to its vast consumer market. The price? Not just cash, but commitments to build local research hubs, transfer valuable technology, or store sensitive data within national borders. It's a modern echo of trading a unique asset (market access, like silk) for a desired capability (advanced tech, like powerful horses).

The Rare Earth Gambit: Today, certain nations hold near-monopolies on rare earth elements, the essential vitamins for our digital age – vital for everything from smartphones to missile guidance systems. This control isn't just economic; it's geopolitical leverage. Access to these minerals could potentially be bartered not just for currency, but for political concessions, strategic partnerships, or favorable deals in other sectors, mirroring China's ancient mastery over silk production.

The Silk-for-Horse trade, therefore, is far more than a historical footnote. It's a timeless lesson carved onto the vast landscape of Eurasia. It reveals how nations, driven by fear, ambition, and the fundamental need for security, have always practiced a form of high-stakes barter, turning unique resources into instruments of power. The shimmer of silk and the thunder of hooves weren't just goods changing hands; they were the very sinews of empire, defense, and diplomacy – a strategic ballet whose steps are still mirrored in the complex resource politics of our own time.

The Human Thread: How the Sogdians Stitched Worlds Together (And Why We Still Need Their Kind)

Forget crisp maps and neat borders. Picture the ancient world as a vast, breathing landscape – deserts that shimmered under unforgiving suns, mountains that clawed at the sky, forests dense with secrets. Connecting these realms wasn't magic, but something far more remarkable: people. Specifically, people willing to gamble everything on the horizon, the tireless weavers of trade who carried not just goods, but understanding, across daunting voids. And among these, the Sogdians weren't just participants; for centuries, they were the pulse.

Imagine stepping into their shoes. Born in the fertile embrace of Samarkand and Bukhara – the heartlands that became modern Uzbekistan and Tajikistan – you weren't just a farmer or a craftsman. You were poised at the planet's crossroads. East met West right outside your door, a constant hum of possibility. The Sogdians didn't just stumble into trade; they mastered it, breathing its rhythms between the 4th and 8th centuries CE. Think of Panjikent, not as archaeological ruins, but as a bustling city alive with the clatter of workshops and the sharp negotiations of the marketplace – a society geared for the road.

Their true genius? They were chameleons of commerce. Standing between the empires of China, India, Persia, and Byzantium, they learned the languages, the customs, the feel of different cultures. Found scribbled on documents unearthed dusty miles away in Turpan and Dunhuang, their own script dances alongside Chinese characters and Turkic notes – proof of lives lived fluently between worlds. This wasn't just business; it was radical empathy turned into an art form.

Carrying silk, jade, fragrant musk, or fragile glass across continents wasn't just about loading a camel. It was a high-stakes tightrope walk. How do you trade when one town uses silver coins, the next prefers barter, and the one after that deals in bolts of silk? The Sogdians figured it out. We glimpse their anxieties and triumphs in faded letters sent home – complaining about unreliable agents, celebrating a good deal, mourning devastating losses. These aren't just historical artifacts; they're whispers from real people managing incredible risks, possessing an almost intuitive grasp of faraway desires and the logistics to satisfy them. Forget spreadsheets; this was gut instinct, hard-won experience, and an encyclopedic knowledge of shifting sands, both literal and economic.

But perhaps their most profound creation, more valuable than any jewel, was trust. In a world without international courts or instant communication, how did you ensure the person you met in a distant oasis wouldn't simply vanish with your goods? The Sogdians built their own safety nets. They scattered like seeds, planting tight-knit communities in vital hubs across Eurasia. These weren't just settlements; they were islands of familiarity in a sea of strangeness. Shared roots, family ties, sometimes a common faith (though they embraced many – Zoroastrianism, Buddhism, Christianity, Manichaeism), created invisible threads of obligation and support. Need a place to stay? A loan? Reliable news about bandits or market gluts? Your fellow Sogdians were your lifeline. They were masters of the "space between," transforming the terrifying vulnerability of the stranger into the reliable comfort of the network, making the impossible distances feel, somehow, manageable.

Does this sound ancient? Look around. The spirit of the Sogdians is alive and kicking:

Think of the global supply chain managers, wrestling with customs forms, shipping containers, and volatile fuel prices. They don't just move boxes; they orchestrate a dizzying ballet across borders, their success built on reliability – a modern echo of the Sogdian promise to deliver.

Consider the cross-cultural business consultant, hired to navigate the delicate nuances of a deal in Tokyo or Dubai. They translate not just words, but unspoken rules, gestures, expectations – they are the human bridges ensuring minds meet as well as markets, fostering understanding just as the Sogdians did.

Look at the digital marketplaces – your Amazons, your Alibabas. They connect a seller in a small town in Vietnam with a buyer in London who would never otherwise meet. How? By building digital trust through reviews, secure payments, and dispute resolution – a vast, algorithm-driven version of the Sogdian network, built on the same fundamental need for reliable connection.

The Sogdians teach us that connection isn't automatic. It's built. It requires courage, adaptability, multilingual fluency (in languages and cultures), and above all, the patient, essential art of building trust. They were more than merchants; they were the sinews of a connected world, the human thread that held the sprawling tapestry together. Their story isn't just history; it's a timeless lesson in how we bridge divides and, ultimately, find ways to understand each other across any distance.

Beyond the Map: Blood, Dust, and Dreams on the Silk Road

Forget the neat lines drawn on museum maps. Picture the Silk Road not as a route, but as a living, breathing network – veins pulsing across the heart of continents. It wasn't drawn with ink, but etched by countless footsteps into brutal deserts like the Taklamakan, a place whose name whispers "you go in, you don't come out," and carved over the Goliathan shoulders of the Pamir mountains, the "Roof of the World." This wasn't a journey for the faint of heart. It demanded more than strong legs and a thirst for exotic goods [Source: Frankopan, P. (2015). The Silk Roads: A New History of the World]. It demanded grit, ingenuity, and a web of trust fragile as silk itself, especially when your payment might be a bale of goods, not a handful of silver.

Imagine the relief, bone-deep and soul-soothing, of spotting a caravanserai after weeks battling relentless sun or biting wind. These weren't just inns; they were fortresses of humanity against the wild. Standing defiant against the vast emptiness, places like the grand Ribat-i Malik in Uzbekistan rose from the earth [Source: Stark, S. (2012). Archaeology of the Central Asian Oases and Silk Road]. Picture thick, protective walls, a single, watchful gate swinging open to reveal a bustling courtyard – a sudden explosion of life. The air thick with the smell of camels, dung, cooking fires, and exotic spices. The clamor of a dozen languages bargaining, sharing news, warning of bandits or praising a newly peaceful stretch of road [Source: Hillenbrand, R. (1994). Islamic Architecture: Form, Function, and Meaning]. Spaced roughly a day's hard trek apart (30-40 kilometers), these weren't accidental shelters; they were calculated anchors, promises of safety built into the very fabric of the journey [Source: Knobloch, E. (2001). Monuments of Central Asia].

And between these stone havens? The oases, emerald jewels flung across landscapes starved for life. Places like Turpan or the legendary Dunhuang weren't mere watering holes; they were miracles coaxed from the earth by human genius. Think of the qanat systems – hidden rivers channeled underground, whispering life beneath the scorching sand, triumphs of engineering that kept the desert at bay [Source: Beaumont, P., et al. (Eds.). (1989). Qanat, Kariz and Khattara]. These weren't just stops; they were vital organs of the Silk Road – farms bursting with provisions, chaotic marketplaces, administrative outposts, and vibrant, messy crucibles where monks debated scripture while merchants haggled over bolts of silk [Source: Whitfield, S. (2004). The Silk Road: Trade, Travel, War and Faith]. The oases were the path, dictating where life, and therefore trade, could possibly flow.

But stone walls and water weren't enough. You needed order, or at least, the idea of order. Great empires – the Han, Tang, Kushans, Sasanians, and later, the formidable Mongols – cast long shadows that sometimes meant safety [Source: Di Cosmo, N. (2002). Ancient China and Its Enemies]. Periods like the Pax Sinica or Pax Mongolica weren't guarantees, but they offered a chance, a possibility of passage less fraught with peril. Garrisons stood watch, travel permits offered a thin shield of authority, and diplomatic missions, blending politics with profit, tried to smooth the way [Source: Hansen, V. (2012). The Silk Road: A New History]. Reading the journals of travelers like the devout Chinese monks Faxian and Xuanzang, or the wide-eyed Marco Polo, is to feel their anxieties, their encounters with suspicious guards, treacherous terrains, and the fragile political webs they navigated [Source: Polo, M. (trans. Yule, H. & Cordier, H.). (1903). The Book of Ser Marco Polo].

In a world often built on barter and a bewildering array of coins, how did you manage risk? You relied on the most potent, yet invisible, infrastructure: trust. This wasn't abstract; it was woven from shared bloodlines, hometown connections, or the common tongue of faith. Think of the legendary Sogdian merchants, whose networks stretched for thousands of miles, built on reputation and kinship [Source: de la Vaissière, É. (2005). Sogdian Traders]. A handshake deal in Samarkand might be honored months later in Chang'an because your cousin vouched for you. Information – about a treacherous pass, a greedy official, or a trustworthy agent – was currency as valuable as gold. Risk was rarely shouldered alone. Merchants pooled their goods, their fates tied together in the shared venture of a single caravan. Traveling in large, armed groups wasn't just practical; it was essential, a rolling fortress against predators human and animal. The caravanserai itself nurtured this – strangers huddled around a fire, sharing stories and dangers, becoming temporary allies, forging bonds for the perilous road ahead [Source: Archaeological analysis suggesting communal defense].

Echoes in Our Modern World:

This ancient rhythm of risk, connection, and infrastructure still beats today, just clad in different materials:

Cathedrals of Commerce: Stand inside a massive logistics hub like Dubai's Jebel Ali Free Zone (JAFZA). It's a modern caravanserai writ large – secure, regulated, a place where global goods pause, are stored, and rerouted. The scale is industrial, but the function – a safe node in a vast network – is timeless.

Digital Handshakes: Those complex international trade agreements (WTO, USMCA, RCEP)? They're the digital descendants of imperial decrees and diplomatic treaties,

aiming to tame the chaos of borders, standardize rules, and offer paths for resolving disputes – reducing the "danger" for today's merchant-multinationals.
Mapping Modern Dangers: When companies frantically reroute shipments due to a pandemic, a blocked canal, or geopolitical tension, they're engaging in the same fundamental risk management as Silk Road traders scanning the horizon for threats. Today's tools are satellite tracking, geopolitical analysis, and insurance policies, but the core anxiety – ensuring the goods get through – is identical. They're mapping the safest "oases" and "routes" in a volatile global landscape.
Old Roads, New Ambitions: China's vast Belt and Road Initiative (BRI) isn't subtle; it deliberately invokes the ghost of the ancient Silk Road. Building ports, railways, and pipelines is a modern echo of establishing caravanserais and securing routes, a grand, geopolitical gamble on the power of infrastructure to shape trade and influence, facing challenges remarkably similar to those encountered by empires past.

Ultimately, the Silk Road wasn't just about silk, spices, or gold. It was a testament to human resilience, our irrepressible need to connect, trade, and explore, even across the most daunting landscapes. It was built not just on stone and water, but on courage, ingenuity, whispered warnings, and the fragile, essential human currency of trust. It was, and remains, a story about us.

Unequal Exchanges: Barter in the Crucible of Colonialism

The Whispers of Worth: When Worlds Offer Gifts

It wasn't just trade, not like we think of ticking off items on a list. It was a conversation started in a language no one fully understood, spoken through beaver pelts and iron pots. For a visitor from across the Great Water, offering a knife might have been a simple transaction – value for value, done. But for the person receiving it, whose world was woven with threads of kinship and shared obligation, that knife might have felt like the start of a relationship, a promise whispered across the cultural divide. Think of the confusion: "Is this a gift requiring one in return later?" "Is this an alliance?" "Or is it just... a knife?" The mismatch wasn't just about goods; it was about the meaning embedded within the exchange, a chasm hidden beneath the surface of the offered items. We glimpse these misunderstandings in the stiff letters sent back to European monarchs and the faded ink of traders' journals, reading between the lines of calculated profit and genuine bewilderment.

The Shock of the New: Metal Sings, Glass Shines

Then came the novelty – the sheer, electrifying newness of it all. Imagine the heft, the impossible edge of a steel axe head landing in a hand accustomed only to patiently shaped stone. Suddenly, the ancient rhythm of felling trees is shattered, replaced by a speed that must have felt like sorcery. That axe, perhaps traded for furs considered abundant, wasn't just a tool; it was a revolution humming in the palm, a fact etched into the earth where archaeologists later find these metal marvels carefully integrated into traditional toolkits.

And the beads! Cheap European glass, yet they arrived shimmering with the allure of the unknown, catching light like captured stars. They found their way into intricate patterns, sometimes taking the place of treasured shells painstakingly gathered and worked over generations. Why? Because they were different, rare (at first), and perhaps held a whisper of the power of the people who brought them. They weren't just ornaments; they were status, mystery, beauty from another reality, a story hinted at in the patterns on preserved artifacts and echoed in the fragmented memories passed down through Indigenous voices.

The Slow Shift: From Wonder to Want

But the sparkle couldn't last. Wonder has a half-life. The initial excitement, the high value placed on furs or knowledge exchanged for these dazzling objects, began to fade as ships arrived more regularly, laden with duplicates. The exotic became commonplace, the value recalculated. We see this cold arithmetic unfold in the meticulous, emotionless ledgers kept at trading posts, where the "price" of a beaver pelt slowly deflates over time.

The most chilling shift came with firearms. First, perhaps, a terrifying curiosity – loud, smoky, powerful. But soon, a grim necessity. Not just for hunting, where their efficiency began to unravel the delicate balance of local ecosystems (imagine the silence falling over streams once bustling with beaver), but for survival. As neighbours acquired these weapons, refusing them meant vulnerability. Suddenly, access to guns, to the powder, the lead, the vital repairs, became a lifeline – a lifeline held firmly by the European suppliers. This wasn't exchange anymore; it was dependence, a tightening knot.

The most tragic chapter? Land. Vast territories, sacred hunting grounds, ancestral homes – signed away in treaties for piles of goods. Blankets, tools, beads, perhaps impressive at the moment, but measured against the irreversible loss of the land itself? It was a transaction weighted with devastating inequality, a story told in the stark language of deeds and the enduring sorrow of dispossession.

Think of the voyageurs paddling deeper into the North American wilderness, their canoes laden with goods that would fuel both alliances and devastating wars like the Beaver Wars. Think of the Spanish demanding gold in the Caribbean, offering trinkets that seemed magical until the true cost became terrifyingly clear.

These first handshakes, these tentative offerings across the beach, were more than simple barter. They were the complex, often heartbreaking, opening scenes of a drama that reshaped continents, economies, and the very understanding of what holds value. They were dialogues begun in mutual curiosity, distorted by misunderstanding, and ultimately weaponized, leaving echoes of inequality and loss that resonate powerfully even today.

From the Circle of Sharing to the Pull of the Market: A Story Etched in Fur

Imagine a world woven from relationships – not just between people, but with the rustling forest, the flowing river, the watchful beaver. Before the tall ships ghosted onto the horizon, life for many Indigenous communities across North America beat to a rhythm of need, respect, and reciprocity. Hunting wasn't just about filling bellies; it was a conversation with the spirits of the animals, a way to strengthen the bonds of community through sharing the bounty. Knowledge wasn't stored in books, but in the whispers of elders, the patterns of the seasons, the sacred understanding that taking too much today meant emptiness tomorrow. Trade happened, yes, but it often felt more like building bridges than striking bargains – gifts exchanged to seal friendships, alliances cemented over shared resources. It was a circle, sustained by balance.

Then, across the vast water, a tremor began – a fashion craze in faraway Europe. Suddenly, the beaver, that clever architect of wetlands, wasn't just a respected part of the ecosystem, a source of sustenance. It became gold. Soft, felted gold for hats perched on European heads. This distant hunger sent ripples across the ocean, landing on North American shores with the force of a tidal wave.

The newcomers arrived bearing wonders: iron kettles that gleamed brighter and heated faster than traditional pots, steel knives with an edge sharper than any stone, guns that spoke with thunder and changed the very nature of hunting and conflict, colourful cloths, and yes, liquids that could steal thought and spirit. At first, it seemed like an invitation, an exciting exchange. Trade furs, receive marvels. Who wouldn't be drawn to tools that eased labour, to items unlike anything seen before?

But this new embrace had sharp edges. The rhythm of life began to change. The hunt shifted focus. It wasn't just about the community's needs anymore, but about satisfying the ceaseless appetite of strangers across the sea. The trap line became less about respectful harvest and more about maximizing yield. Ancient knowledge about sustainable practices strained against the pull of immediate reward – the reward being those coveted European goods. The meticulous ledgers kept in remote trading posts tell a stark tale: a rising tide of pelts flowing out, a growing reliance on goods flowing in.

The land itself felt the strain. The beaver, once ubiquitous, vanished from creek after creek, forest after forest. Its dams crumbled, wetlands dried, and the intricate web of life it supported frayed. This wasn't the careful tending of generations past; it was a feverish rush, stripping the land bare. Imagine the silence settling over waterways that once teemed with life, the growing anxiety as familiar hunting grounds yielded less and less. Millions of beaver lives were traded for felt hats, leaving ecological wounds that would take centuries to heal, if ever.

And the hunger for trade wasn't just for kettles and knives; it was for advantage, for power. As beaver became scarce, tensions flared. Old rivalries sharpened, and new ones ignited as groups pushed into neighbours' territories, desperate for the furs that bought firearms and secured alliances with the powerful newcomers. The "Beaver Wars" weren't just about territory; they were a tragic symptom of this new, competitive world, fueled by European trade goods and amplified by the deadly efficiency of the guns they provided. Brotherhood turned to bloodshed over access to the trading post.

Perhaps the deepest change was the slow coiling of dependency. The sharp axe replaced the stone tool, the musket replaced the bow for many essential tasks, woven cloth replaced painstakingly prepared hides. Traditional skills, honed over millennia, began to fade like old memories. Communities found their fortunes tied not to the health of their local ecosystem, but to the fickle whims of fashion in London or Paris. A dip in beaver prices overseas could mean hardship and hunger back home. Worse, the trading posts often operated on credit, ensnaring hunters in a cycle of debt – always needing more furs to pay off last season's supplies, digging deeper into the resource deficit, deeper into reliance. The thread of trade had become a chain.

The Echoes Today:

This story, etched in the history of the fur trade, isn't confined to the past. Its ghost lingers, its patterns reappear in new forms:

Think of the Amazon rainforest, where the global craving for cheap beef, soy, or timber fuels the chainsaws and fires. Indigenous communities there watch their ancestral forests disappear, their way of life threatened, facing violence and displacement as their homes become commodities for distant markets – the same pressure, a different resource.

Look to the Arctic, where the melting ice unlocks pathways to oil, gas, and minerals. The world's hunger for energy and resources rushes north, promising economic boons but threatening fragile ecosystems vital for Inuit subsistence hunting and fishing, potentially creating a new reliance on volatile global prices – the boom-and-bust cycle returns.

Consider the cobalt mines in the Congo. Our insatiable demand for batteries to power smartphones and electric cars fuels a brutal scramble. Communities face horrific conditions, environmental ruin, and violent conflict over control of the mines, reaping little benefit from the wealth extracted from their land – a modern, devastating resource rush driven by global desire.

The story of the fur trade is a profound, human lesson about what happens when local lives and intricate ecosystems become entangled with powerful, external demands without safeguards. It's a story of transformation, loss, and the enduring challenge of balancing need with sustainability, autonomy with interconnection – a story that continues to unfold, urging us to listen to its echoes today.

The Devil's Bargain: Everyday Goods and the Theft of Humanity

Imagine the docks, not just as loading zones, but as stages where the soul of the world was being tragically rewritten. Liverpool, Nantes, Lisbon – names now etched in history, but then, they were merely points of departure for ships laden not just with cargo, but with the seeds of unimaginable suffering. This wasn't just trade; it was a monstrous alchemy, transforming bolts of cloth, barrels of rum, and stacks of iron bars into the currency that would purchase human lives. Forget sterile economic terms; this was the brutal arithmetic of dehumanization, the first, aching verse in the ballad of the triangular trade.

Think of the textiles. Picture the explosion of color – vibrant Indian cottons, sturdy British wools, fine Dutch linens – unfurling under the African sun. These weren't just fabrics. In the hands of coastal traders and powerful elites, they were shimmering symbols of status, intricate weaves of power and influence. A beautiful cloth could adorn a body, signify rank, or seal a deal. Yet, carried in the holds of slave ships, these same beautiful threads became insidious tools. Each yard measured out wasn't just length, it was leverage; each pattern, a potential price tag on a person's future. Shipping manifests, those cold lists of calicoes and checks, read less like inventory and more like the shopping lists for stolen generations. The soft touch of cotton became complicit in the harsh reality of chains.

Then, the firearms. Feel the cold weight of a musket, smell the sharp tang of gunpowder. These weren't simply weapons; they were engines of disruption, deliberately introduced to shatter existing balances. European powers poured them onto the continent, knowing full well the consequence. Access to guns became the key to power, the means for one group to dominate another, to hunt people like animals. The horrifying irony hangs heavy: the very tools used to capture individuals were obtained by selling those same individuals. Each shot fired in a raid echoed the transaction that brought the weapon, a deadly feedback loop fueled by greed and gunpowder, turning communities against each other in a desperate scramble for the means of their own, and others', destruction.

Consider the alcohol. Rum, brandy, gin – flowing not just down throats, but through the cracks of negotiation, smoothing the path for monstrous agreements. Imagine it being poured, a lubricant for the mechanisms of the slave trade, sometimes clouding judgment, other times offered as a routine part of the grim package deal. Merchant diaries whisper of casks rolled ashore, used to break deadlocks, to toast bargains sealed in human misery. It was a liquid facilitator, often distilled from the sugar harvested by enslaved hands elsewhere – a bitter ouroboros, consuming itself to perpetuate the cycle.

And the metals. Iron bars, uniform and heavy, stacked like ominous ingots. Valued for their potential – tools to till the earth, blades for defense – they became, on the coast, a crude standard for measuring human worth. How many bars of inert metal equaled the life, the potential, the spirit of a man, woman, or child? Copper and brass, gleaming manillas clasped onto wrists not as adornment, but as units of account in this ledger of loss. Archaeology unearths these objects from the soil of trading posts, silent witnesses to the moment potential was traded for bondage, the moment a human being was appraised like raw material.

This wasn't merely an exchange; it was a fundamental violation of personhood. The core horror lies in the calculation itself: that a life could be equated to a specific assortment of goods. A human heart weighed against gunpowder kegs. A person's future balanced against bolts of cloth. The meticulous records kept by merchants weren't just bookkeeping; they were the chilling documentation of humanity being rendered itemized, stripped bare, and entered into a column of profit and loss.

The journey didn't end there. These goods, the price of stolen lives, set in motion the horrors of the Middle Passage. The people purchased with cloth and guns were then forced onto plantations, their stolen labor producing the sugar, tobacco, and cotton that flowed back to Europe, generating staggering wealth. This wealth, in turn, financed the very factories that produced more textiles, more guns, more metal bars to fuel the next voyage, the next purchase, the next wave of devastation. A relentless, demonic engine powered by manufactured goods and human suffering.

The Echoes in Our World:

This history isn't sealed in the past. Its ghost lingers, its mechanisms find new forms:

The Shadow of Unequal Value: Look at the labels on your clothes, the components in your phone. Does the price reflect the human effort involved? The historical precedent of valuing African lives cheaply against European goods finds a distorted echo in modern supply chains where immense profit is built on minimally compensated labor in unseen corners of the world. The geography changes, the goods change, but the chilling math of unequal exchange persists.

The Curse of Endowment: Think of nations rich in oil or diamonds, yet plagued by conflict and stunted development. The influx of European goods, especially weapons, often warped African economies, stifling local craft and fostering dependency. It mirrors the modern "resource curse," where singular wealth fuels power struggles and hinders diversified growth, a legacy of economies shaped by external demand rather than internal potential.

The Unsettled Ledger: The immense wealth that built empires and financed industrial revolutions was inextricably linked to the goods-for-people trade. The prosperity enjoyed in parts of the world today carries the imprint of that historical extraction. Conversely, the deep economic disparities and developmental hurdles faced in parts of Africa are, in part, the enduring consequence of centuries of lost human capital and socio-political disruption fueled by this trade. The conversation about reparations and global inequality isn't just about the past; it's about acknowledging how the value assigned to cloth, guns, and iron centuries ago continues to shape the fortunes of nations and peoples today.

Those seemingly ordinary objects – cloth, guns, alcohol, metal – were far more than simple cargo. They were the keys that unlocked a Pandora's Box of dehumanization, the tangible facilitators of the transatlantic slave trade. Their legacy isn't just rust and faded fabric; it's woven into the very fabric of our modern world, a chilling reminder of the devastating consequences when humanity itself becomes a commodity.

The Handshake That Stole the Future: How Colonial Trade Rewired the World and Left Us Shaking

It might have started softly, a curious glance across a shore, the clink of metal tools offered for unfamiliar food, beads shimmering against fur. A simple exchange, perhaps. But look closer, and that first barter wasn't just a trade; it was the opening scene of a global drama whose final act is still being written, often in tears and frustration. Those early encounters, seemingly innocent, were the quiet insertion of a key into the intricate locks of local life, a key that would be turned, ruthlessly, to reshape entire societies for distant profits. The story isn't just about economics; it's about the ghosts of silenced looms, the taste of unfamiliar hunger on lands that once fed their own, and the echoes of power imbalances that still make the ground beneath our feet feel uneven.

Imagine the vibrant hum of a pre-colonial marketplace – the intricate weave of Indian cloth admired across continents, the gleam of African metalwork born from generations of skill. These weren't quaint crafts; they were engines of local economies, sources of pride and livelihood. Then came the empires, armed not just with guns, but with tariffs, restrictions, and an insatiable hunger for markets. Suddenly, the hands that wove magic were forced idle. Think of India, where threads that once clothed the world were deliberately tangled and cut by British policy, making way for the relentless march of Lancashire cotton. This wasn't fair competition; it was a targeted dismantling, a silencing of local ingenuity to ensure the colonizer's factories roared loudest. The legacy? Skills vanished like smoke, local wealth evaporated, and the colourful tapestry of diverse economies faded into a monochrome dictated from afar.

At the same time, the land itself was conscripted. Vast stretches of earth, once nurturing a variety of crops that fed local families, were transformed into giant factories under the sun, dedicated to a single, foreign craving. Sugar here, rubber there, cocoa spilling from West Africa, cotton carpeting Egypt – all feeding the relentless appetite of the colonizer's industries. Yes, money changed hands, but it flowed overwhelmingly towards colonial coffers, leaving the local people trapped in an economic straitjacket. They were forced to grow what they couldn't eat, their fortunes now tethered to the unpredictable whims of markets thousands of miles away. Imagine Ghana, its fate still swaying precariously with every dip and rise in the global price of cocoa – a vulnerability sewn into its soil during colonial times. This wasn't just about exports; it was about risk. Fields dedicated to cash crops couldn't grow food, biodiversity withered, and the earth itself grew tired, mirroring the exhaustion of its people. Local plates grew emptier as distant tables groaned.

This economic surgery cut deep into the social soul. The very ground people stood on was redefined, communal ties severed as land was carved up, privatized, and handed over for plantations. Families were uprooted, becoming strangers in their own ancestral homes, creating waves of landlessness and desperation. To work these new enterprises – the plantations, the mines – people were often forced, indentured, or drawn into cycles of low-wage labour that shattered old social structures and kinship bonds. Picture the 'coolie' trade, the harsh realities of mine compounds – these weren't just labour systems; they were human tragedies that carved new, painful hierarchies. New figures emerged, intermediaries who navigated the colonial world, often benefiting while their communities fractured. Traditional leaders found their authority hollowed out or twisted to serve foreign masters. These weren't just administrative changes; they were fault lines etched into society, breeding tensions and inequalities that continue to rumble long after the colonizers officially left.

Thinkers have tried to map these enduring scars. Dependency Theory paints a stark picture: a world divided into a wealthy 'core' and a struggling 'periphery' – former colonies still caught in a cycle of exporting raw materials cheap and importing finished goods dear, an echo of the old power dynamic. Postcolonial Studies looks deeper, exploring the psychological wounds, the ways economic chains are tangled with cultural legacies and lingering feelings of 'us' and 'them'.

And this isn't ancient history; it's the news headlines. Look at the Congo (DRC), overflowing with minerals vital for our smartphones and electric cars, yet trapped in cycles of conflict and exploitation rooted in the brutal Belgian extraction of its wealth. The treasure in the ground becomes a curse, not a blessing. Look at the Caribbean islands, often reliant on the fickle waves of tourism or the vestiges of plantation crops, their economic horizons still framed by choices made centuries ago under a colonial sun.

So, that initial handshake? It morphed into a grip that squeezed the life out of local industries, rerouted the flow of wealth, reshaped the land, and reordered society itself. It left behind economies often precariously balanced on one or two commodities, vulnerable social fabrics, and a deep-seated sense of chasing a future always just out of reach. Understanding this painful inheritance isn't just an academic exercise; it's crucial to recognizing the ghosts of empire that still walk among us, shaping global inequalities and the profound challenge many nations face in truly claiming their economic independence. The echoes linger, demanding we listen.

When Money Dies: Barter as a Lifeline in Historical Crises

When Money Became a Ghost: Surviving the Weimar Nightmare of 1923

Forget flickering black-and-white images for a moment. Imagine feeling 1923. Not as a historian, but as a Berliner, a mother, a factory worker. Imagine the air thick not just with coal smoke, but with a gnawing, escalating fear. Because the money in your pocket, the very symbol of your labor, your security, your future – it was becoming a ghost.

The Great War had bled the nation, and the crushing weight of reparations demanded by the victors pressed down like a physical force. The government, desperate, reached for the printing press, unleashing a flood of Papiermarks utterly disconnected from anything real [Source: Feldman, G. D. (1993)]. It wasn't just inflation; it was hyperinflation, a runaway train gathering terrifying speed. The Mark didn't just fall; it evaporated. Picture this: the few coins you clutched walking into the bakery might buy less bread by the time you reached the counter, minutes later [Source: Evans, R. J. (2003) - capturing anecdotal accounts]. Trust, the invisible thread holding commerce together, simply snapped [Source: Bresciani-Turroni, C. (1937)].

By November, the numbers became meaningless, surreal jokes whispered in disbelief: 4.2 trillion Marks for a single American dollar [Fact/Figure: Fergusson, A. (2010)]. Trillion. A number so vast it felt like dust. People literally hauled wheelbarrows overflowing with this phantom cash just to buy basic groceries, a grotesque parody of wealth [Source: Evans, R. J. (2003)].

What do you do when money dies? You remember something older. Something primal. You trade.

This wasn't some organized return to a simpler time. It was a chaotic, frantic scramble for survival – Tauschhandel, the Germans called it, the barter trade born of desperation [Source: Fischer, C. (2010)]. Personal diaries and hushed family stories from the time paint the picture: life stripped bare [Source: Referenced in Fergusson (2010); Hughes, M. L. (1988)]. Suddenly, your grandmother's treasured necklace wasn't a memory; it was potential potatoes. That painting on the wall? Maybe it could become coal to fight off the freezing winter nights [Source: Peukert, D. J. K. (1992); Personal diaries referenced in Fergusson (2010)]. Food – flour, meat, eggs – became the new gold standard. Fuel was life itself.

Skills became currency too. Imagine the plumber, not asking for Marks, but for bread to fix the leak that threatened to flood your apartment. The doctor treating a sick child, not for a fee, but for a desperately needed sack of coal. The teacher imparting knowledge, hoping for a warm meal in return [Source: Anecdotal evidence from memoirs]. Farmers, holding the key to sustenance, briefly held a strange power over city dwellers, though the crumbling infrastructure and spreading chaos meant no one was truly safe [Source: Holtfrerich, C.-L. (1986)].

The damage wasn't just economic; it tore at the soul of society. The solid middle class, the bedrock of stability, saw their life savings, their pensions, turn to worthless paper overnight. Imagine the bitterness, the feeling of utter betrayal [***Source: Fergusson (2010)***]. The invisible glue of trust dissolved, replaced by the acid of suspicion. Did your neighbour have food? Could you trust anyone? Crime inevitably festered in the shadows of desperation [Source: Contemporary newspaper reports]. The psychological toll was immense – a constant hum of anxiety, a crushing weight of hopelessness. This wasn't just poverty; it was the erosion of dignity, creating fertile ground for the dark ideologies that promised easy answers and scapegoats [***Source: Peukert (1992); Evans (2003)***].

Echoes in Our Time:

Don't mistake 1923 for a dusty relic. It's a ghost that still walks.

Modern Nightmares: Ask someone who lived through Zimbabwe in the late 2000s or Venezuela in recent years. They'll tell you similar stories: worthless currency, the desperate hunt for stable foreign cash (like the US dollar), the return to bartering basics, the same social fraying [Source: IMF, World Bank reports, journalistic accounts]. The human response to monetary collapse is tragically universal.

Lessons Learned (or Ignored?): Governments and banks study Weimar like doctors study plagues, hoping to understand the warning signs, the tipping points, striving for policies that prevent such a catastrophe [Source: Macroeconomic textbooks]. It remains the ultimate cautionary tale against fiscal recklessness.

Whispers of Alternatives: While vastly different, the spectre of Weimar sometimes surfaces in debates about cryptocurrencies. The idea of money outside government control resonates with the fear of hyperinflation, though digital currencies carry their own volatile risks [Source: Financial tech discussions].

The Weimar Republic's descent into the barter nightmare of 1923 is more than history; it's a raw, human testament to how fragile our systems are. It shows what happens when faith in the shared symbol of value – money – disintegrates, forcing people back to the most fundamental exchanges, trading pieces of their lives just to survive another day. It's a haunting lesson etched not in economic charts, but in human memory and enduring fear.

The Great Cash Vanishing Act

In this chaotic dawn, money itself seemed to melt away. Imagine holding a fistful of rubles, only to feel their worth evaporating like mist as hyperinflation roared. Official banks, once cogs in the mighty state machine, seized up like rusted gears. Trying to pay another company through the official system was like shouting into a void – choked by a paralyzing knot of debts nobody could settle. The arteries of commerce were clogged solid. At the same time, the invisible threads that once stitched the planned economy together – linking Siberian mines to Ukrainian factories to Baltic ports – snapped, leaving businesses utterly stranded. How do you get rubber for tires when the supplier vanished? How do you sell tractors when your usual buyer can't pay, and the state isn't buying anymore?

The Rise of the Great Barter Chains: A Dance of Desperation

Out of this wreckage, something strange and unwieldy bloomed: Enterprise Barter. But erase the image of simple swaps – Farmer Giles trading eggs for blacksmith shoes. This was something far grander, more desperate, and infinitely more complex. Think vast, sprawling daisy chains of obligation stretching across thousands of miles and dozens of companies.

Imagine a steel mill, unable to pay its workers in cash that held value. So, perhaps workers received partial payment in… saucepans, or tires, or whatever the mill could get its hands on. They'd then hawk these goods in local markets for food. The mill, needing coal to fire its furnaces, might trade a shipment of steel girders to a mining conglomerate. But the miners didn't need steel; they needed electricity. So, the steel mill's "credit" from the mine might be transferred to the regional power company. The power company, perpetually owed money by everyone, might grudgingly accept this "steel credit" as partial payment against the mill's massive outstanding electricity bill, or perhaps offset it against its own taxes owed to a cash-starved government. Sometimes, energy itself – gas from giants like Gazprom – became a kind of shadow currency, traded down the line for pipes, food, or construction services.

It was a breathtakingly convoluted ballet of survival. IOUs, tax offsets, deliveries of goods acting as payment – anything went. Numbers from the time are staggering: estimates suggest over half, perhaps even up to 70%, of industrial transactions in Russia became non-monetary. It wasn't a fringe activity; it was the economy for vast swathes of industry.

The High Price of Just Staying Afloat

This wasn't efficiency; it was life support, cobbled together with metaphorical duct tape and hope. Barter, especially on this scale, is brutally inefficient. How do you even agree on the "price" of steel girders versus coal versus electricity versus tax debt when actual money prices are meaningless? Deals were often arbitrary, driven by desperation, leading to immense hidden losses.

The sheer effort involved was enormous – endless searching for partners willing to take your goods and offer something you (or someone down the chain) needed; labyrinthine negotiations; the constant fear that someone, somewhere in the chain, would default, bringing the whole precarious structure crashing down.

Worse, this "virtual economy," as economists Clifford Gaddy and Barry Ickes brilliantly termed it, was a world of smoke and mirrors. It hid which companies were truly viable and which were corporate zombies, kept alive only by these non-cash exchanges and the state's reluctance (or inability) to enforce bankruptcy. It allowed massive tax evasion and obscured the real financial picture, making genuine restructuring nearly impossible. Necessary pain – the closure of hopelessly inefficient Soviet-era behemoths – was endlessly deferred.

Snapshots from the Twilight Zone:

The Energy Giants' Strange Role: Imagine Gazprom, a global energy titan, forced to accept payment for its invaluable natural gas not in dollars or rubles, but in trainloads of manufactured goods it didn't necessarily want, or complex debt-swaps with regional governments. They became reluctant barter hubs.

Ukraine's Industrial Maze: Picture huge Ukrainian steel plants, cut off from old supply lines and starved of cash, bartering finished steel across borders for Russian coal or ore, navigating a bewildering cross-republic web of trade just to keep the furnaces lit.

The "Tolling" Sidestep: Envision a Western company shipping raw materials (like alumina for making aluminum) to a Russian smelter, paying the processing fees (often covered by the smelter's own barter deals for electricity), and then taking the finished metal away as payment. 1 It was a way to use Russian industrial capacity while completely bypassing the collapsing local monetary system.

A Legacy of Distortion

The great post-Soviet barter wave was a raw, powerful testament to human ingenuity in the face of systemic collapse. It arguably prevented an even more catastrophic implosion, keeping millions employed and factories churning, however inefficiently.

But it was a survival mechanism born of profound sickness – the death of money, the failure of institutions, the disintegration of infrastructure. It cast a long shadow, creating a distorted, opaque "virtual" layer over the economy that took years of painful stabilization and market reforms to finally peel back. It was the economy holding its breath, waiting for real money and real markets to return from a terrifying void.

When the World Holds its Breath: Finding Life in the Cracks of Total War

Imagine the sky heavy, not just with clouds, but with the constant thrum of fear. Total war isn't just fought on distant battlefields; it creeps under doorways, settles in kitchens, and gnaws at the edges of everyday life. The predictable rhythm of buying bread, mending shoes, sharing a cup of tea – it fractures. Governments try to impose order with ration books, neat little stamps meant to promise fairness [Overy, R.J.]. But paper promises often leave stomachs aching and spirits low [Zweiniger-Bargielowska, I.]. The official ration might keep you breathing, but it rarely warms the soul or acknowledges the small cravings that make us human – a child's longing for something sweet, a grandparent's need for familiar comfort [Collingham, L.].

Into this void, this chasm between what was given and what was desperately needed, bloomed an ancient human instinct: the art of the trade. Barter wasn't just resurrected; it became a vibrant, sometimes dangerous, lifeline, a testament to human ingenuity when the usual systems fail [Hinton, J.].

Forget simple swaps. This was lifeblood exchanged in whispers, a complex dance happening just out of sight of patrolling eyes. Diaries and hushed family stories tell the tale [Summerfield & Peniston-Bird, C.]. Picture this: the earthy smell of potatoes, hoarded from a precious garden patch, traded under the cover of dusk for the jewel-like sweetness of a neighbour's last jar of jam – an exchange built on trust stronger than any law [echoed in Slavnikova, O.]. Or the skilled hands of a plumber, coaxing life back into frozen pipes, rewarded not with flimsy cash, but with the potent luxury of a few cigarettes. The seamstress, patching worn-thin clothes, might earn precious eggs, her needle weaving threads of survival as much as fabric [Stargardt, N.]. These weren't just transactions; they were threads binding communities together, though sometimes pulled taut by suspicion or perceived unfairness [Noakes, J.].

Some things became more than just things. They were keys, unlocking doors official rations couldn't budge. Cigarettes, those small paper tubes, transformed into a near-universal language of need and temporary escape across a fractured continent [Mazower, M.]. Their value wasn't just the nicotine buzz; it was their easy tradeability, a pocket-sized promise that could be exchanged for almost anything [Buchheim & Scherner, J.]. Imagine the clink of a hidden bottle of cognac in France, the sharp scent of schnapps in Germany, the almost mythical aroma of real coffee, the decadent melt of forbidden chocolate, the simple dignity of a bar of soap, or the sheer, shimmering hope embodied in a pair of silk stockings [Cobb, M.]. These weren't mere luxuries; they were sparks of defiance, reminders of a life worth fighting for, worth trading for. And fuel – coal, wood, petrol – was pure power, the ability to stave off the biting cold that seeped through cracked window panes, a bargaining chip of immense weight [Barber & Harrison, M.].

Of course, this hidden world danced dangerously close to the illegal black market. Trading rationed goods? Strictly forbidden. Getting caught meant fines, shame, even prison [Fearnley, C.]. Propaganda posters screamed warnings, painting traders as traitors harming the boys at the front [Ministry of Information (UK)]. Yet, especially in cities shattered by bombs or strangled by occupation, this shadow economy wasn't just present; it thrived [insights from Boldorf & Okazaki, T.]. For countless ordinary people, this wasn't about greed. It was about finding medicine for a feverish child when the chemist was empty. It was about scraping together enough calories to see the next sunrise when official supplies had vanished [Beevor, A.]. It was about survival, pure and simple.

Think of Leningrad (1941-1944), besieged and starving. There, the grim reality stripped barter down to its terrifying core. A beloved book, a family heirloom, the very furniture you sat on – traded for a crust of bread, perhaps bulked out with sawdust. Value wasn't measured in gold, but in heartbeats, in the raw calories needed to fend off death itself [Reid, A.].

Or consider Occupied France, where "Système D" became a national motto – the art of "getting by." It was a mix of hidden gardens, hushed neighbourhood exchanges, and daring black market deals, a whole society learning to navigate the treacherous currents of scarcity and oppression with cunning and resilience [Fogg, S. L.].

Even in Britain, spared invasion but squeezed by austerity, the "spivs" and under-the-counter deals flourished. A farmer might slip a neighbour some eggs, bypassing the ministry man. A city dweller might treasure an illicit petrol coupon or trade favours for precious nylons, tiny rebellions against the drabness and restriction [Zweiniger-Bargielowska, I.].

So, no, wartime barter wasn't just an economic footnote. It was the pulse of humanity refusing to be extinguished. It was born of broken systems and desperate needs, a complex web woven from neighbourly kindness, calculated risk, and sheer, stubborn ingenuity. It showed people finding ways to connect, to care, to endure, and to hold onto fragments of normalcy when the world itself seemed bent on tearing everything apart. To understand the war means understanding these hidden exchanges, these quiet acts of survival that kept the human spirit alive in the darkest of times.

Putting a Price on Pain: When Money Suddenly Vanishes

Imagine waking up tomorrow, and the cash in your wallet is suddenly just paper. Not worthless, maybe, but unusable. That's the chaotic heart of a large-scale demonetization – a monetary earthquake that sends shockwaves through everyone's lives. Trying to figure out the real cost of such an event is like trying to measure a ghost. It's not just about counting the vanished notes; it's about capturing the frustration, the lost chances, the sheer inefficiency that ripples outwards when the familiar flow of money suddenly clots. It's the economic equivalent of hitting the emergency brake on a speeding train – you know it's jarring, but measuring every bump, every missed connection, every frayed nerve? That's the real puzzle.

Economists have long understood why money is so vital. Think back to basics: without cash, you're stuck in the clumsy world of barter. Need bread, but only have chickens? Good luck finding a baker who desperately needs a chicken right now. Money is the magic wand that makes these awkward swaps disappear, letting us trade smoothly and quickly. Theories with fancy names like 'Money-in-the-Utility' or 'Cash-in-Advance' basically say the same thing in math: not having enough usable cash makes life harder. It either stops you from buying what you need or forces you to waste precious time and energy just figuring out how to trade, shrinking everyone's slice of the pie. It's like forcing everyone to run a marathon with their shoelaces tied together – possible, perhaps, but slow, painful, and deeply inefficient.

So, what happens when this isn't just theory? India's 2016 demonetization became a real-time, high-stakes experiment watched around the globe. Trying to untangle its effects is like detective work at a chaotic crime scene. You see the obvious clues: the national economic heartbeat (GDP growth) took a noticeable dip – some experts said by a little, some by a lot, maybe half a percent, maybe even over two percent knocked off in the immediate aftermath. Pinning it just on the note ban is tough, like blaming one raindrop for a flood, but the timing was stark. You saw people stop buying things, especially bigger items or in rural areas where cash was king. Why? Simple: if you can't get the cash, you can't spend it. Empty shops, postponed purchases – that's lost business for sellers and frustration for buyers, a direct hit to well-being.

Researchers got creative trying to capture the freeze. Some looked at satellite images of nighttime lights – a clever proxy for economic buzz. In areas with fewer banks, the lights dimmed noticeably, suggesting the cash drought literally slowed down activity. Others zoomed in on the vast "informal" economy – the street vendors, the small workshops, the daily wage earners – who rely almost entirely on cash. Suddenly, they were forced into awkward IOUs, delayed payments, revived barter systems, or simply stopped trading. It wasn't quite swapping goats for services, but it was a huge step backward, forcing people to rely on trust, memory, and cumbersome workarounds. Think of the hours lost queuing at banks, the deals that fell through, the sheer anxiety – that's the "welfare loss" economists talk about, felt not in spreadsheets, but in daily life.

History even chimes in. Look at places hit by runaway inflation, like Germany after World War I. When the official money became worthless, people scrambled for alternatives – cigarettes became currency, dollars were hoarded, barter crept back in. It shows a universal truth: when the money system breaks, people find ways to cope, but always at a steep cost to efficiency and ease.

In the end, putting a single, neat number on the cost of yanking money out of an economy is incredibly tricky. It's like trying to measure the ripples in a pond long after the stone has sunk. But while the exact figures are debated, the story told by both economic theory and real-world observation is clear: disrupting the flow of money is like starving an economy of oxygen. It introduces grit into the gears of commerce, slows everything down, and leaves a trail of lost opportunities and heightened frustration. The true cost isn't just a percentage point of GDP; it's measured in the friction felt in every transaction, the anxiety in every empty wallet, the drag on the rhythm of everyday life.

Echoes of Collapse: Contemporary Barter in the Face of Economic Failure

When Money Became a Ghost: Argentina's Great Barter Uprising

Imagine a nation holding its breath. Argentina, around the turn of the millennium, wasn't just facing an economic downturn; it was staring into an abyss. Years of policies that sounded good on paper, like tying the peso rigidly to the mighty US dollar, had cracked under pressure, leading to a spectacular crash. Debt spiralled, the government defaulted, and then came the final, brutal blow: the corralito. Suddenly, the banks slammed their doors shut. Your own money, the little you had left, was trapped behind glass, unreachable.

Cash didn't just become scarce; it became a ghost haunting the streets. Official unemployment figures screamed past 20%, but that number couldn't capture the gnawing emptiness in millions of stomachs, the quiet desperation in homes where parents couldn't buy milk or mend shoes. The formal economy, the one with paychecks and price tags, had simply vanished for vast swathes of the population.

But Argentinians are survivors. From the cracks in the broken system, something incredible began to sprout. Small, neighbourly swaps – a bag of home-grown tomatoes for fixing a leaky tap – that had always existed on the fringes, suddenly exploded. This wasn't just about saving a few pesos; this was about survival. These scattered exchanges coalesced, organised, and morphed into the vibrant, sprawling phenomenon of the clubes de trueque.

Think of it: school gyms, church halls, dusty public squares transforming, perhaps just once a week, into bustling marketplaces unlike any other. These weren't shops, but nodos – nodes in a vast, invisible network woven by necessity. People weren't just customers or sellers; they became prosumidores, a beautifully Argentine term capturing the essence – you were both a producer and a consumer. You brought what you had – perhaps freshly baked bread, knitted baby clothes, hours of plumbing skills, or even a song – and you looked for what you needed.

Direct swapping is tricky, though. What if the baker didn't need his plumbing fixed today? The genius of the trueque networks was the birth of their own money: the crédito. Little slips of paper, often printed locally, sometimes looking barely official, became the lifeblood of this alternative economy. They weren't backed by gold or government decree, but by something far more powerful in that moment: mutual trust and shared need. You "sold" your knitted sweaters for créditos, then used those créditos to get flour from the baker or a haircut from the stylist. It was a handshake turned into currency, a promise circulating within the community. Major networks tried to bring order to this paper tide, but its heart remained fiercely local and, at times, beautifully chaotic.

At their zenith in 2002, estimates suggest millions – maybe up to six million Argentinians – were breathing life into these networks. Imagine the scale! This wasn't a marginal activity; it was a parallel nation, operating on trust and ingenuity. The trueque became far more than a marketplace. It was the social safety net the government couldn't provide, woven by calloused hands and determined spirits. It was where you didn't just find food, but solidarity. Where sharing skills wasn't just barter, but connection. In the face of national despair, the ferias buzzed with a different energy: the dignity of providing, the warmth of community, the quiet resilience of people refusing to be broken. They were reclaiming agency, helping each other stand tall when everything else was falling apart.

And this Argentinian story isn't just a relic of a painful past. It's a living testament, an echo resonating across the globe whenever and wherever traditional economic systems falter. Think of the LETS schemes in the UK or Japan, the spontaneous barter networks that emerged during Greece's debt agony, even modern digital platforms exploring community currencies. They all carry whispers of the trueque.

Born from the harsh bite of necessity, the clubes de trueque showed the world the incredible power of grassroots innovation. They remind us that when the familiar structures crumble, human beings possess an extraordinary capacity to self-organise, to build something new from the rubble, fuelled not by profit, but by the simple, profound need to care for one another. It's a story etched not just in economic textbooks, but in the enduring strength of the human spirit.

Where Money Turned to Dust: Surviving Venezuela's Economic Ghost

Imagine waking up not to the sun, but to the gnawing dread that the paper in your wallet is dissolving, turning to phantom dust before your eyes. This wasn't a nightmare. This was life in Venezuela, beginning its sharp descent in the mid-2010s, as the bolívar, the nation's currency, became a ghost haunting the marketplace. Picture this: needing a backpack, not a wallet, overflowing with bills just to buy lunch – a reality etched into the memory of millions (as documented by countless news reports showing the sheer absurdity of cash volume). Savings evaporated like morning mist. Salaries became cruel jokes whispered at the end of the month.

But humans are rivers, not rocks. Faced with an economic cliff, Venezuelans didn't just fall; they carved new channels. The oldest form of commerce, the one whispered in our ancestral blood, roared back to life: barter. Suddenly, the coastal towns pulsed with ancient rhythms. A fisherman wouldn't sell his gleaming catch for fading bolívares; he'd trade it directly for the glint of cooking oil, the promise of a hot meal. A teacher, her official pay rendered insulting, would offer the treasure of knowledge – math lessons, history stories – in exchange for precious antibiotics or a bag of rice. In neighbourhoods, garden vegetables, nurtured with scarce water and hope, became currency for diapers; a mechanic's skill could earn a family enough flour for a week. This wasn't a quaint throwback; it was raw survival, a human network humming beneath the collapsing official system, a testament to the fact that value lies in need and skill when formal money fails (echoing anthropological studies on crisis economies).

At the same time, another phantom crept in, but this one had weight: the US dollar. First, it was a whisper, a preference for big-ticket items, a way to anchor savings against the bolívar's freefall. Then, it was a steady current, fueled by the lifeline of remittances – dollars sent like digital messages in a bottle from sons, daughters, cousins who had joined the swelling diaspora, their hard currency landing directly into kitchens and neighbourhood shops (a flow tracked by global institutions). The dollar wasn't just stable; it felt real.

This green tide birthed new landscapes. Small shops, the bodegones, bloomed like defiant flowers in a barren field, their shelves stocked with imported goods – Colombian milk, Brazilian sugar, American toothpaste – priced almost exclusively in the forbidden, yet essential, dollars (a phenomenon widely reported locally). Near the borders, frontiers blurred not just geographically but economically. Places like Cúcuta in Colombia became vital arteries, informal markets buzzing with cross-border trade, where pesos and dollars were king, offering access to medicines and food that had vanished from Venezuelan shelves (as observed by border-monitoring groups). A family in Táchira might live almost entirely outside the bolívar's orbit, their survival depending on dollars earned informally or sent from abroad, spent across the border.

The dollar even went digital. In Caracas cafes or for freelance gigs, transactions zipped through platforms like Zelle, virtual wallets becoming as common as worn-out leather ones. Yet, this created a new divide. Those with smartphones, international bank contacts, or tech-savvy relatives could navigate this parallel economy. But the farmer in the remote Andes, the elderly couple without connections – they were often stranded, relying on the tangible, sometimes difficult, dance of barter or the increasingly scarce bolívares. Access became a currency in itself.

Venezuela's story of hyperinflation isn't just about economic charts that spike into the stratosphere. It's about the fisherman judging the worth of his catch against a bottle of oil. It's the anxious glance at a phone confirming a Zelle transfer. It's the heavy backpack of near-worthless cash. It's a breathtaking, sometimes heartbreaking, mosaic of human ingenuity forged in the fire of collapse – a blend of ancient practices and digital streams, of cross-border hustle and neighbourly exchange. It showcases incredible resilience, the fierce human will to endure. But it also reveals an economy fractured, etched with the deep lines of inequality drawn by access to a foreign greenback, a daily struggle navigated under the long shadow of monetary ruin. The ghost of the bolívar might be fainter now, but the landscape it haunted remains profoundly changed.

When the Coins Fall Silent: The Human Heartbeat of Barter in Crisis

Imagine the unthinkable: the ATMs are dark, the market stalls empty, the familiar rustle of banknotes replaced by an unnerving silence. When the scaffolding of our modern economy buckles under war, disaster, or financial ruin, an ancient rhythm often resurfaces – the simple, direct exchange of barter. It's the oldest marketplace known to humankind, reborn not from choice, but from the stark landscape of necessity.

Is this return to trading a grandmother's quilt for a bag of flour a testament to our resilient spirit, a neighbourly dance of mutual support? Or is it a shadow play, highlighting the darkness of systemic collapse and the raw edge of human desperation? The truth, felt in empty stomachs and seen in helping hands, is rarely simple.

The Spark of Connection in the Rubble

In the dust of crisis, barter can be a lifeline woven from trust. When official channels clog or vanish, neighbours rediscover each other. Suddenly, the retired plumber's skill is worth more than gold; the baker sharing starter becomes a community linchpin. We see the quiet strength of shared survival. Think of hands, calloused from clearing debris after a storm, accepting a warm meal offered by someone whose roof they helped patch. Think of online neighbourhood groups during lockdowns, transforming into digital trading posts where a bag of hoarded yeast could be swapped for help getting groceries to someone isolated.

These aren't just transactions; they are affirmations. In moments of profound powerlessness, trading a skill, a possession, a moment of time restores a sense of agency, a feeling of worth beyond what defunct money can measure. It's the pulse of community breathing life back into itself, stitch by painful stitch, proving that our connections can be currency too. These networks, built on reciprocity and understanding, are like campfires in a storm – small points of warmth and light against a vast darkness.

The Cold Calculus of Need

But let's not romanticize the edge of survival. The widespread need to barter is often a glaring symptom of a deeper sickness – the failure of the systems meant to protect us. When money becomes meaningless paper, barter isn't an alternative lifestyle choice; it's the last resort before the void. Remember Argentina's clubes de trueque? Born from economic implosion, they were initially hailed as symbols of grassroots power. Yet, these vast networks eventually groaned under their own weight, struggling with fairness, efficiency, and the sheer difficulty of matching infinite needs with finite haves. Millions participated, not out of revolutionary zeal, but out of the desperate need to simply get through the day.

This desperation creates a dangerous imbalance. The person holding the last tin of medicine or litre of fuel suddenly wields immense power. The exchange can become less about mutual aid and more about raw leverage. Is it truly a fair trade when a family heirloom, steeped in memory, is handed over for a few days' worth of food? Ethical lines blur when one party negotiates from the cliff-edge of starvation. The inherent inefficiency – that maddening search for someone who needs exactly what you have and has exactly what you need – adds another layer of friction and frustration. Barter struggles to handle the complex needs of a modern life suddenly stripped bare.

Beyond the Trade: Seeking Solid Ground

Barter in crisis is a mirror reflecting both the best and the most challenging aspects of humanity under pressure. It can be a beautiful testament to our innate drive to connect, share, and survive together. It can light sparks of solidarity in the darkest hours.

However, its very necessity is often a profound indictment of broken structures. It's a temporary, often leaky, lifeboat, not the shore. While the resilience shown in these makeshift markets is deeply human and vital for immediate survival, it can also mask the deepening cracks of inequality and the hard truths of exploitation born from scarcity.

Ultimately, while we must honour and support the spirit of mutual aid that barter represents, the real goal isn't just to get better at trading goods when the system fails. It's to demand and rebuild systems that don't force us back to the barest, most precarious forms of exchange simply to endure. True recovery isn't just surviving the storm; it's finding our way back to solid ground.

The Ghost in the Marketplace: When Pockets Empty and Pixels Fill the Void

Imagine the sound of an economy grinding to a halt. It's not a loud crash, but a slow, unnerving silence. The familiar jingle of coins fades. The crisp rustle of banknotes becomes a memory. In these moments of tremor, when the structures we built wobble, humanity does something instinctive, something ancient: we look to each other. We reach back to the oldest form of commerce – the simple, honest swap. "I have eggs, you have flour. Let's trade."

But the old ways, born of tight-knit villages and shared paths, stumble in our sprawling modern world. How do you find the one person miles away who needs your spare blankets and happens to have the medicine you desperately seek? The village square is too small, the whispers too quiet. Barter, in its raw form, is a dance of improbable luck – finding that perfect match, that "double coincidence," feels like searching for a single star in a cloudy night sky.

Then comes the flicker. The unexpected lifeline held in the palm of your hand. The phone.

That little slab of glass and circuitry, often dismissed as a distraction, becomes a powerful prosthetic for a broken economy. It's the digital crutch we never knew we'd need, bridging the chasms left when money fails. Suddenly, the village square is boundless. A simple text message, a quick call – "Anyone have spare batteries? Can trade coffee" – leaps across neighborhoods, across towns. That 80% mobile phone penetration projected for Sub-Saharan Africa isn't just a statistic; it's millions of potential handshakes, millions of possible trades, bypassing potholes and broken supply chains. Geography shrinks. Hope expands.

Social media and messaging apps become the new bustling bazaars, humming with urgent whispers turned into digital shouts. Facebook groups, WhatsApp channels, Telegram threads – they morph into vibrant, chaotic marketplaces born of necessity. Picture it: a constant stream of posts, a tapestry woven from needs and haves.

"Need baby formula, can offer mending services." "Anyone trading gasoline for potatoes near West Gate?" "Found extra antibiotics – looking for fresh vegetables." It's the pulse of a community refusing to go dark, documented not in dusty ledgers, but in the endless scroll. Remember Greece, staring into the abyss of debt? It wasn't just politicians debating; it was ordinary people firing up their phones, organizing swaps, building webs of mutual aid, proving resilience isn't just about enduring, but about adapting.

And what about trust, that fragile currency essential for any exchange? Bartering with strangers is fraught with risk. But technology offers a strange, digital facsimile of community. Shared connections in a group, a profile picture, a history of posts, perhaps even informal vouching systems ("Yeah, Maria's good for her word") – these pixels build a fragile, temporary bridge of trust. It's not the sturdy bond of lifelong neighbors, perhaps, but enough to make the leap, enough to trade. Ad hoc digital tribes form, united by the shared goal of getting through today.

Look at Venezuela, grappling with hyperinflation that turned cash into confetti. WhatsApp wasn't just for chatting; it became the tool. Countless groups sprung up, coordinating intricate barters for everything imaginable – food, medicine, car parts, skills. Sometimes digital payments zipped across borders (using platforms like Zelle), but the core principle remained: direct human exchange, midwifed by readily available tech. We even see specialized apps pop up occasionally, trying to formalize these digital swap-meets.

This isn't just about technology helping. It's fundamentally rewriting the script of survival. It's the ghost in the machine of the informal economy, a network humming beneath the surface, powered by simple devices and human ingenuity. When the main lights flicker and die, these digital embers glow, allowing communities to find warmth, share resources, and navigate the darkness, one digitally-assisted swap at a time. It's the oldest human instinct meeting the newest tools – a testament to our stubborn, creative drive to connect and endure.

The Corporate Swap Meet: Organized Business-to-Business Barter

Beyond Swapping Sandwiches: The Birth of the Barter Hub

Remember trying to trade your lunch back in school? You had peanut butter, wanted pizza, but the pizza kid wanted cookies? That's the "double coincidence of wants," and it's a headache. Now, imagine a smart, central hub – a kind of financial matchmaker for businesses. That's your modern barter exchange. It's not just a record-keeper; it's the bustling town square where businesses connect, even if they don't directly need what the other has right now. This hub cleverly sidesteps that whole "you want what I have, I want what you have" logjam. You bring your surplus (goods or services) to the party, and the hub takes note.

Enter the Connectors: Your Barter Wingman (or Wingwoman!)

This isn't just automated software; there's a crucial human element: the Trade Broker. Think of them less as stuffy account managers and more as your personal business matchmaker, networker, and opportunity scout, all rolled into one. These are the folks pounding the pavement (metaphorically, mostly!), inviting diverse businesses into the fold. They're the ones who really listen – understanding what makes your business tick, what you desperately need, and what you're brilliant at providing. They're the energetic connectors whispering, "Hey, Printer Pete, meet Marketing Mary – I think you two could make magic happen." They don't just hope trades happen; they actively grease the wheels, nudge connections, and help structure deals that make everyone smile. A good broker is the spark plug igniting the whole barter engine.

Meet the "Barter Bucks": Your In-House Currency

So, you "sold" your excess stuff or services through the exchange. Cha-ching! But instead of cash, your account fills up with "Trade Credits" or "Trade Dollars." Think of it as the exchange's exclusive club currency. It's simple: usually, one trade dollar equals one regular dollar ($1 TD = $1 USD, for example), keeping things straightforward. Here's the magic: you earned those credits from Company A, but you don't need anything from them. No problem! You can spin around and spend those credits with any other member – Company B for web design, Company C for catering, Company D for window cleaning. It completely disconnects the need for a direct swap. That printing company earning $5,000 in trade credits? They might splash $3k on a radio ad campaign and $2k on getting their office carpets cleaned, all without touching their cash reserves. It's like having a secret stash specifically for offsetting everyday expenses.

Widening the Circle: When Local Goes Global (Almost!)

A single exchange is great, but what if you need something really specific, or your local network is tapped out? Enter the big leagues: networks like IRTA (International Reciprocal Trade Association) and NATE (National Association of Trade Exchanges). Picture these as the super-connectors, linking hundreds of individual barter exchanges like an intricate highway system. Suddenly, your membership in a Chicago exchange might let you use your hard-earned trade credits to snag a deal with a business in London, Miami, or Toronto, all thanks to these umbrella organizations. It blows the doors wide open, exponentially increasing the variety of things you can buy and sell, making your membership infinitely more powerful.

We're talking billions circulating through these interconnected networks – it's a huge, hidden economy.

Where the Rubber Meets the Road: Barter in Action

This isn't just theory; businesses are doing this every single day:

Got Empty Airwaves or Pages? Radio stations, magazines, websites often have ad space they haven't sold. Instead of letting it vanish, they trade it for plumbing repairs, printing, or even hotel stays for their sales team. That unsold spot becomes new computers!

Quiet Hotel Tonight? An empty hotel room earns zero dollars. Through barter, that same room can be "sold" for trade credits, which the hotel then uses to pay for landscaping, marketing brochures, or staff appreciation dinners. Lost revenue becomes valuable services.

Warehouse Overflowing? Got last season's widget or too much inventory? Instead of selling it for pennies on the dollar in a fire sale, trade it through the exchange for its full value in credits. Use those credits to buy things you actually need – accounting help, delivery services, you name it. Turning dust-collectors into assets!

Skills to Spare? Lawyers, consultants, designers, tech gurus – if you have billable hours or expertise, you can trade it. Get marketing help, pay for corporate events, or even score travel opportunities, all by leveraging your professional skills within the network. Your brainpower buys the next team lunch.

The Bottom Line:

Forget the old-school notion of swapping chickens for firewood. Today's corporate barter is a sophisticated, dynamic ecosystem. Powered by dedicated brokers, fueled by flexible trade credits, and amplified by vast networks, it's a potent strategic tool. It lets businesses keep more cash in the bank, find customers they never would have reached, turn excess into opportunity, and operate with a level of financial agility that the cash-only world often misses. It's about trading smarter, not just harder.

Beyond the Buzzwords: Why Swapping Stuff is Still Seriously Smart Business

Think barter's just a throwback, something folks did before fancy money systems? Think again. In today's hyper-speed, cash-obsessed world, the ancient art of the trade is making a seriously slick comeback. It's not about desperation; it's about strategy. It's corporate barter, and it's less dusty relic, more secret weapon.

1. Keeping the Cash Flowing: The Lifeblood Stays Home

Cash is king, queen, and the whole royal court in business. It pays the team, keeps the lights on, fuels the next big idea. But what if you could get exactly what you need – maybe that killer ad campaign, essential supplies, or crucial travel – without actually spending that precious cash? That's barter's first magic trick. It's like saying, "I need that, but instead of draining my bank account, I'll trade you something I have." Suddenly, there's breathing room. Especially for smaller businesses or those pouring every penny into growth, swapping services or goods keeps the operational heart beating strong, even when the cash flow feels tight. Imagine the relief of getting vital marketing exposure by trading products you already have, instead of writing a check you were sweating over.

2. The Warehouse Whisperer: Turning Dead Stock into Dynamic Assets

Picture that back room or warehouse corner: boxes of last season's gizmos, perfectly good stuff that's just... sitting there. It's not just gathering dust; it's tying up money and costing you more every day (storage, insurance, the slow march to worthlessness). Slashing prices feels like waving a white flag and hurts your brand's image. Writing it off is just admitting defeat. But barter? Barter flips the script. It's like financial alchemy: transforming that potential loss, that pile of "yesterday," into something valuable today. That surplus stock, traded at its real value (or close to it!), suddenly becomes credits for things you were going to pay cash for – maybe media spots, new office furniture, or even team travel. Companies have literally turned mountains of unwanted inventory into prime-time advertising, swapping potential write-offs for market presence.

3. Filling the Empty Seats: Waking Up Idle Capacity

An empty hotel room tonight, a vacant seat on tomorrow's flight, an unsold ad slot in this week's magazine – what do they have in common? Once the moment passes, that potential income vanishes forever. Poof. It's the curse of "perishable" services. The cost of filling that one extra room or seat is often tiny compared to the cost of keeping the lights on anyway. Barter steps in like a resourceful ghostbuster, capturing that evaporating value. Hotels swap empty rooms for new linens or staff training. Airlines trade seats for catering services or billboard space. Media outlets exchange unsold airtime or column inches for everything from company cars to IT support. It's the ultimate "waste not, want not," turning zero-revenue silence into a tangible offset for planned expenses.

4. The Secret Handshake: Finding Customers Off the Beaten Path

Joining a barter network is like getting keys to a hidden marketplace. Suddenly, you're visible to a whole new crowd of potential customers – other businesses in the network – folks you might never have reached with your usual ads. Often, the business you get through barter is pure bonus business; sales you simply wouldn't have made otherwise. Think of the local restaurant that joins a trade exchange. Suddenly, employees from the print shop, the marketing agency, and the IT firm down the street are coming in for lunch, paying with trade credits. Those are tables filled, connections made, all sparked by the barter network. Sometimes, you might even sweeten a deal for a cash customer by accepting part-payment in trade, using barter as that clever little nudge to win them over.

5. The Sum is Greater: Weaving a Stronger Profit Picture

It's not just one thing; it's how these pieces dance together. Save cash here, turn old stock into value there, fill empty slots over yonder, welcome new faces through the door… it all feeds the bottom line. By smartly sidestepping cash expenses for things you need anyway, and by conjuring value out of assets that were underperforming or idle, barter becomes a quiet contributor to better profitability. It's not about randomly swapping; it's about intentionally using trade to offset budgeted costs or generate genuinely new income streams.

So, the next time you hear "barter," don't picture ancient marketplaces. Picture sharp, modern businesses playing the game smarter, using an age-old tool with fresh, strategic eyes to conserve cash, unlock hidden value, and build a more resilient, resourceful, and ultimately, more profitable operation. It's the oldest trick in the book, refreshed for the digital age.

The Ghost of Cash: Why Your Swap Isn't Free

You might think trading your killer graphic design skills for a year's worth of gourmet coffee is just a clever, cash-free arrangement. Sweet deal, right? Well, yes and no. The biggest plot twist for many is that Uncle Sam (or your local tax authority) sees that exchange almost exactly like cold, hard cash changing hands. The IRS, for instance, is crystal clear: the "fair market value" (FMV) of whatever you received counts as income. Period. It's baked right into the definition of income – basically, if you got value, it counts, whether it arrived as a check, a service, or a mountain of artisanal cheese [Source: IRS Topic No. 420; 26 U.S. Code § 61]. Slipping these non-cash deals under the radar? It's a common temptation, but also a major reason folks find themselves facing audits and penalties down the line [Source: TIGTA reports often flag this].

The Tricky Tango of "Fair Market Value"

So, everything hinges on this "Fair Market Value." What magical number is that? Simply put, it's the price your bartered item or service would likely fetch if sold openly, where both buyer and seller are reasonably informed and neither is desperate [Source: IRS Publication 561 principles]. Easy enough if you're trading, say, $1,000 of standard website maintenance for $1,000 of standard accounting services – the market price is usually obvious.

But what about trading your unique, hand-carved furniture for a custom software build? Or swapping a series of specialized consulting sessions for prime advertising space? Suddenly, "fair value" gets slippery. It can feel more like an art than a science. This is where things get dicey. Accounting gurus often debate the best ways to pin down value for these unique swaps, stressing that solid proof and sometimes even professional appraisals are key [Source: Accounting journals like Journal of Accountancy on ASC 845]. If you lowball the value (intentionally or not) and the tax authorities disagree, they can assign their value, often leading to a bigger tax bill plus some painful penalties. It's a common theme in tax court battles [Source: e.g., Baker v. Commissioner].

Confess Your Barter Sins: The Reporting Ritual

Whether you like it or not, you've got to report your barter bounty. Businesses using organized "barter exchanges" – platforms where you trade using special credits or "trade dollars" – have it spelled out for them. These exchanges must send out a Form 1099-B to members and the IRS, detailing the value of trades made [Source: IRS Instructions for Form 1099-B]. And we're not talking pocket change; these exchanges move billions globally each year [Source: IRTA stats].

Even if you're just doing a direct, one-on-one swap with another business – the bakery trading cakes for marketing help, for example – the obligation doesn't vanish. Both sides need to declare the FMV of what they received as income on their regular tax forms (like Schedule C or Form 1120) [Source: IRS Publication 525]. Think of it as acknowledging the economic reality of the transaction.

Beyond the Tax Man: Armor Up with Agreements & Records

Taxes are the big bear, but don't forget the other potential pitfalls. To avoid future "he said, she said" arguments about what was really agreed upon, get it in writing! A clear barter agreement acts like a pre-nup for your trade. Spell out exactly what's being exchanged, the agreed-upon value (and how you reached it!), when it will happen, and any guarantees. Many business disputes that end up in court involve hazy non-cash deals where expectations didn't match [Source: Business law case studies].

And alongside that agreement? Keep meticulous records. Note the date, who was involved, what was traded, and why you valued it the way you did. This isn't just fussy paperwork; it's your evidence, your shield, if auditors come knocking or disagreements arise. Even formal accounting rules dictate how these non-monetary trades should appear on your financial statements, aiming for clarity and honesty [Source: FASB ASC 845].

Bringing it Home: Barter in the Wild

The Main Street Swap: Our baker trades $500 worth of delicious cakes (her standard price) for $500 worth of social media buzz (the marketer's standard package). Both report $500 income. Simple, clean, documented. If the marketer deducts her own business expenses but doesn't report the cake income, that mismatch could raise red flags.

The Corporate Credit Shuffle: A hotel dumps $10,000 worth of empty rooms (valued fairly) into a barter exchange, getting $10,000 in trade credits. They spend those credits on advertising from a media outlet also in the exchange. Come tax time, boom, both the hotel and the media company get a 1099-B from the exchange showing $10,000 in barter activity. The IRS is kept in the loop automatically.

The Bottom Line?

Bartering feels wonderfully old-school, a clever way to conserve cash. But in the modern world, it demands modern respect. Treat it with the same seriousness you'd give a cash transaction. Nail down the value, report it honestly, document everything, and get clear agreements. Do that, and you can enjoy the benefits of the swap without the sting of unexpected trouble later. Barter smart, not just hard.

Is Corporate Barter Just Business CPR, or Is It Learning to Dance?

Picture this: Corporate barter isn't some dusty artifact pulled out only when the economy gasps for air. Sure, it shines as a financial lifeboat when cash suddenly becomes painfully shy. When recessions loom, businesses cleverly turn to barter, transforming warehouses full of unsold gizmos or empty appointment slots into vital advertising space or essential supplies. It's the ultimate act of resourcefulness – spinning straw (unsold inventory) into gold (needed services) without cracking open the emergency cash box. Studies confirm this – like clockwork, interest in barter ticks up when the financial forecast looks grey. It's the savvy business equivalent of finding forgotten money in an old coat pocket, just when you need it most.

But here's where it gets interesting: Barter isn't just waiting for rainy days anymore. It's stepping out even when the sun is shining. Think of it as a secret handshake for smart companies. Need to break into a new market? Offer your services via trade credits. Want to snag a big client? Maybe accepting part-payment in their goods gets your foot in the door. It's becoming a strategic tool for growth, not just survival. The sheer scale – billions swirling around in organized barter exchanges globally even before the pandemic – tells you this is more than just a handful of companies swapping paperclips.

The Real Game Changer? Barter Went Digital, Big Time.

The biggest hurdle for barter used to be finding that perfect match – like business dating in the dark, often needing an expensive broker. Enter the digital revolution. Today, sleek online B2B barter platforms are buzzing marketplaces. Imagine eBay, but instead of cash, businesses are swapping services, inventory, and digital "trade credits." Suddenly, you're not limited to trading with the company next door; you have a whole digital ecosystem of potential partners.

This tech infusion is like giving barter a shot of adrenaline:

Matchmaking Magic: Forget endless phone calls. Algorithms now suggest perfect trading partners based on what you have and what you need. It's faster, smarter, and opens up way more possibilities.

Value Clarity: Figuring out if your surplus widgets are worth their premium website design used to be a headache. Now, data analytics and even AI are stepping in, offering more transparent, real-time valuations. Less guesswork, more fairness.

Trust Turbocharged: Worried about getting your end of the deal? Blockchain technology is peeking around the corner, promising super-secure, automated contracts and transparent tracking of those digital trade credits. Think of it as a digital notary for swaps.

Smooth Operator: From finding partners to tracking balances, these platforms handle the nitty-gritty, making barter accessible even for smaller businesses that previously found it too complex.

Where's the Barter Action Happening?

It's everywhere, often hidden in plain sight:

Media Moguls: Broadcasters and publishers routinely swap unsold ad slots (think empty radio time or website banners) for everything from new office furniture to company cars or vacation packages for staff incentives. Advertisers get exposure without spending cash; media outlets turn empty space into real value.

Hospitality Hustle: Hotels are masters at this, trading empty rooms – a perishable asset if ever there was one – for marketing campaigns, renovation services, or even staff training. Airlines do the same with empty seats.

Inventory Ingenuity: Got last season's fashion or food nearing its sell-by date? Barter networks are lifelines, helping businesses trade this slow-moving stock for essential operating needs like IT support or logistics, avoiding costly write-offs and brand-damaging deep discounts.

So, What's the Verdict? Relic or Revolution?

Let's be real: Cash isn't going anywhere. But corporate barter is definitively shedding its skin as a mere niche survival tactic. Fueled by the constant pressure for financial agility and supercharged by digital platforms that make it slick, efficient, and accessible, it's morphing into something much more dynamic.

It's becoming a sophisticated strategy woven into the fabric of modern B2B dealings – a way to unlock hidden value, conserve precious cash, and gain a competitive edge. While challenges like agreeing on value and navigating tax rules remain, technology is steadily smoothing those bumps.

The future isn't about barter replacing cash. It's about barter taking its rightful place as a smarter, tech-enabled, and growing member of the financial toolkit. Think of it less as an old relic and more as an evolving trend – an ancient concept reborn for the digital age, proving that sometimes the oldest ideas, when reimagined, are the most innovative.

Nations Trading Favors: Government Countertrade and International Relations

Beyond the Swap Meet: Unpacking Countertrade

Think back to ancient times: you have grain, I have tools, we swap. That's barter – simple, direct, but honestly, pretty clunky for today's interconnected world. Countertrade is barter's sophisticated, globe-trotting cousin. It's not just one deal; it's a promise wrapped in a purchase. When a country or company sells something, they agree, right there in the contract, to buy something back. It's a strategic handshake that says, "I'll help you, if you help me."

Why bother with this complexity? Sometimes, cash is tight. A nation might have plenty to offer (resources, manufactured goods) but lack the hard foreign currency needed for big imports. Other times, it's about muscle – big industries like defense or aerospace often involve governments demanding more than just the hardware; they want investment, jobs, and technology for their own people. The big players like the WTO know these deals happen, even if they operate in the grey areas of standard trade rules. And while it's hard to pin down exact numbers (these deals can be quite hush-hush), estimates suggest this intricate web of linked trades accounts for a surprisingly hefty chunk – maybe 5%, maybe even over 20% – of all global commerce.

The Different Flavors of "You Scratch My Back..."

Countertrade isn't a one-size-fits-all strategy. It comes in several distinct forms:

The "I'll Buy Yours if You Buy Mine" Deal (Counter-purchase): This is the most common flavour. Imagine Company A sells machinery to Country B for cold, hard cash. Standard stuff, right? But, attached to that deal is a separate promise: Company A must then buy a certain value of unrelated goods – maybe coffee, textiles, or electronics – from Country B within a set time. It's like saying, "Thanks for buying my tractors; now I'll commit to buying your coffee beans over the next two years." It helps Country B keep its foreign cash reserves healthy and gives its own export industries a guaranteed customer. It's a smart way to crack open new markets or move surplus stock.

The "Pay Me Back With What I Helped You Make" Deal (Buyback/Compensation): This one's about long-term partnership, often involving huge projects. Picture a tech firm building a state-of-the-art chemical plant in a developing nation. Instead of just getting paid upfront, the firm agrees to take its payment (or part of it) over several years in the form of chemicals produced by that very plant. The seller is literally invested in the success of the project they helped build. Their payday depends on the quality and output rolling off the new production line. This is crucial for getting massive infrastructure or technology transfer projects off the ground, especially when initial funding is a hurdle.

The "Big Spender's Sweetener" Deal (Offset Agreements): Welcome to the high-stakes world of government mega-purchases, especially defense and aerospace. When a country spends billions on new fighter jets or transport systems, they often flex their muscles and demand the seller "offset" that huge expense by giving something back to their economy. This isn't just a side agreement; it's often a core requirement. Offsets can be:

Directly Linked: The seller agrees to activities tied to the main purchase. Think: letting local companies build parts for those jets, sharing specific technology, or training local engineers to maintain the equipment. It's about building local capability related to the big buy. Lockheed Martin selling F-35s often involves deals for parts to be made in the buying nation.

Creatively Unrelated (Indirect): Here's where it gets broad. The seller might agree to invest in a completely different local industry (like agriculture tech), buy unrelated local products for their global supply chain, help market the buying country's goods elsewhere, or even fund tourism campaigns! The connection to the original sale might be zero, but the benefit to the buying country's economy is the key. These offset demands can be massive, sometimes even more than the value of the initial contract, showing just how much economic and political leverage they carry.

The Bottom Line

So, while pure barter is a straightforward swap, countertrade is a whole different playbook. It uses money, involves complex contracts, and strategically ties buying and selling together. Whether it's counter-purchase, buyback, or offset, these arrangements are born from real-world needs: managing currency, breaking into markets, transferring technology, or ensuring massive government spending brings broader economic benefits home. It's a dynamic, often hidden, but absolutely vital part of how the world really trades.

Okay, let's breathe some life into this fascinating economic maneuvering. Forget dry policy papers for a moment and think about the tightrope walk many governments face. Why would they deliberately step back into a world that looks like complex barter when cash is king? It's not nostalgia; it's often a hard-nosed strategy born from sheer necessity, a kind of economic judo where you use the weight of limitations to your advantage.

1. When the Global ATM is Empty: The Forex Lifeline

Imagine needing life-saving medicine or critical machinery to keep the lights on, but your nation's wallet – its foreign currency reserves – is perilously thin. Maybe debt is crushing, trade isn't going your way, or sanctions have slammed the door shut. Hard cash like dollars or euros becomes rarer than diamonds. This is where countertrade morphs from a dusty concept into a vital lifeline. As scholars like Hennart observed during crises like the 1980s Latin American debt squeeze, governments grasp countertrade like a life raft. Instead of bleeding precious dollars they don't have, they offer up their own goods or services in exchange for what they desperately need. Think of the former Eastern Bloc nations, often short on globally accepted cash; they cleverly used countertrade to get Western tech and goods, essentially saying, "We'll pay you in products, not paper currency." It's a way to keep importing essentials without digging deeper into a financial hole.

2. Money That Won't Travel: Escaping the Currency Trap

What happens when your national currency is like a movie ticket valid only in one theater? If other countries won't readily accept your rubles, pesos, or rupiahs for payment, you're stuck. Your money isn't "convertible" on the world stage. Countertrade becomes the ingenious escape hatch. It allows a nation to say, "Okay, you don't want our currency? How about our world-class vodka?" This isn't hypothetical – it's the legendary Pepsico-Soviet Union tango! Pepsi craved entry into the vast Soviet market, but the ruble was a no-go internationally. The brilliant solution? Pepsi brought the fizz and the bottling know-how, and in return, got the exclusive right to sell Stolichnaya vodka to the West. It was a masterful swap, turning a non-tradable currency problem into a mutually beneficial trade, all without touching the closed-loop ruble.

3. Finding a Home for Unloved Exports: The Matchmaker Role

Sometimes, a country has plenty of something – maybe mountains of agricultural produce, basic manufactured goods, or commodities facing a global glut – but finding buyers is tough. The global marketplace can be brutal. Here, a government might step in and play matchmaker through countertrade. They might tell a foreign company selling into their country, "Great, we'll buy your turbines, but you must buy an equivalent value of our palm oil (or shoes, or textiles) and find a market for it." Malaysia, for instance, has skillfully woven deals involving its palm oil into contracts for major infrastructure or defense buys, essentially guaranteeing an export channel for a crucial national product. It's a strategic push to keep local industries humming, protect jobs, and sometimes, pry open doors to new markets that wouldn't open otherwise.

4. More Than Just Goods: Trading for Tomorrow's Tech (The Offset Gambit)

This is where countertrade gets really sophisticated, especially in big-ticket government shopping like defense or aerospace. It's called an "offset." Imagine a country buying a fleet of advanced fighter jets. That's a staggering cost. So, the buying government says, "We'll buy your jets, but it comes with strings attached. You need to 'offset' a chunk of this cost by investing here." This isn't just about cash; it's often about knowledge. The deal might require the seller to transfer technology, set up local factories to build components, train local engineers, or fund research labs. As experts in defense economics point out, this is a powerful industrial strategy. Nations like India use these offset policies deliberately, aiming to build their own high-tech industries on the back of major purchases. It's less a simple trade, more a strategic bargain: "Give us your hardware, but also help us learn to build our own future."

5. Building Big Dreams Without Big Cash: Project Financing Magic

How does a nation rich in resources but poor in capital build that massive mine, pipeline, or factory it needs to develop? When traditional loans are out of reach or prohibitively expensive, countertrade, especially "buy-back" deals, offers a path. A foreign company agrees to fund and build the entire project – a huge upfront investment. How do they get paid back? Not in cash, necessarily. Instead, they receive a predetermined share of the project's future output – tons of minerals, barrels of oil, or units of manufactured goods – over many years. It's like saying, "Build us this engine of growth, and we'll pay you back with the very riches it unlocks." Historical deals developing Soviet resources and modern resource-for-infrastructure swaps (like some between China and African nations) run on this very principle: leveraging future potential to finance present-day needs.

So, while it might seem less efficient than swiping a global credit card, countertrade is far from a relic. It's a collection of clever, adaptable tools wielded by governments navigating tricky economic currents. It's about survival, strategic positioning, and sometimes, the only way to turn national needs and resources into global participation. It's the art of the necessary deal.

The Price Tag Has a Shadow: Welcome to the World of Defense Offsets

Imagine this: a nation decides it needs cutting-edge fighter jets, tanks, or missile systems. The price tag is astronomical, enough to make eyes water. But wait, there's a twist in the tale. Before the ink dries on the contract, the buying nation often plays a powerful card: "If we buy your expensive toys," they say to the foreign arms giant, "you've got to promise to spend a hefty chunk of that money right back here, in our country."

That, in essence, is a defense offset. It's not just about buying weapons anymore; it's about leveraging that massive purchase to spark something more back home. Think of it as economic judo – using the weight of a necessary defense purchase to throw open doors for local industry, create jobs for its people, and maybe, just maybe, learn some of the high-tech magic the seller possesses. This isn't some small side bet; offset deals can demand companies reinvest anywhere from 30% to sometimes over 100% of the original contract value back into the buyer's economy. Suddenly, buying missiles becomes a potential engine for national growth.

The Dream: Forging the Future on the Anvil of Defense Spending

Why do nations insist on these complex arrangements? The dream is seductive. Governments see those billions flowing out for foreign jets and think, "How can we capture some of that back? How can we make this unavoidable spending work for us?" The goals are ambitious:

Sparking the Economy: Funnel foreign cash into local businesses, big and small.

Creating Skilled Jobs: Not just assembling widgets, but fostering careers in engineering, advanced manufacturing, and tech.

Borrowing Brilliance (Technology Transfer): This is often the holy grail. The hope is to gain access to critical know-how, moving beyond simply assembling parts ('build-to-print') to actually understanding the design, co-developing new systems, or even launching joint research ventures. It's about learning to fish, not just being given a fish (even if it's a missile-shaped one). The ultimate aim? To build a nation's own muscle in defense and technology, reducing reliance on others down the road.

The Reality Check: Glitter, Grit, and Ghosts in the Machine

But like any dream that sounds too good to be true, the world of offsets is shadowed by skepticism and sharp questions. Critics often whisper (and sometimes shout) that this "economic alchemy" comes at a hidden cost:

The Premium Price: Does negotiating and managing these complex offset deals just inflate the original price of the weapons? Are countries essentially paying extra for benefits that might never fully materialize?

Phantom Jobs & Fuzzy Math: Are the promised jobs real, sustainable careers, or just temporary assembly line gigs that vanish when the project ends? Do they just shuffle workers around, or genuinely grow the national workforce? Measuring the true net benefit is notoriously tricky.

Hand-Me-Down Tech?: Is the technology transferred truly cutting-edge, or is it slightly dated? Sometimes, crucial elements remain a 'black box' – the buyer gets the component but not the deep understanding needed to innovate independently. It might be learning to assemble the puzzle, but never getting the picture on the box lid.

Murky Waters: These massive, complex deals can sometimes lack transparency. Who gets chosen as the local partner? Are the deals fair, or do they create opportunities for corruption?

Stories from the Front Lines

The real world shows this isn't just theory. India's massive Rafale jet deal came with huge offset promises (around half the deal's value!). But the reality got messy, facing probes over whether the commitments were met, how local partners were picked, and if truly valuable technology actually changed hands.

Contrast that with South Korea, often seen as playing a shrewder game. They've strategically used offsets from deals like the F-35 purchase to target specific tech areas, aiming laser-like at building long-term industrial power in aerospace. Countries like Turkey and the UAE have also explicitly woven offsets into grand national strategies, using them as levers to diversify their economies and build homegrown defense industries.

The High-Stakes Gamble

So, defense offsets are far more than financial footnotes. They represent a gamble where national security meets national ambition. For governments, they're a politically potent way to say, "Yes, we're spending billions on defense, but look – it's also building our future!"

But the question lingers: Are they truly effective engines of progress, or just expensive window dressing on colossal arms deals? Do they forge real industrial strength, or merely create an echo of prosperity? The jury is still out, and the results vary wildly, proving that turning defense spending into lasting economic gold remains one of the toughest tricks in the geopolitical playbook.

Trading Without the Tinkle of Coins: The Awkward Dance of Countertrade

Cash is king, right? Simple, clean, universally understood. You give me money, I give you stuff. Easy. But what happens when the king is broke, locked away, or simply not welcome? That's when international trade gets... creative. Enter countertrade – the world's sprawling, sometimes messy, often necessary swap meet.

Imagine it less like a sleek online transaction and more like that complicated multi-person trade you tried to organize in the schoolyard: "I'll give you my sandwich for your comic book, but only if you also get Sarah's cookies for my apple..." It's trade, yes, but with extra steps, extra headaches, and a whole lot of "it depends." This isn't just bartering apples for oranges; it can involve complex deals where jets are traded for promises to build local factories (offsets), or goods are bought now with a commitment to buy other goods back later (counter-purchase, buyback).

Why Even Bother? The Survival Kit Argument

So, if it's such a hassle, why does this seemingly old-fashioned way of doing business persist? Because sometimes, it's the only game in town.

When the Well is Dry: Picture a nation desperate for essential machines or medicine but whose coffers are empty of dollars or euros. Countertrade becomes a lifeline. They can say, "Look, we don't have the cash, but we've got tons of coffee beans, timber, or maybe even skilled labor. Let's make a deal." It's a way to keep the lights on, importing necessities by leveraging what they do have. Think of it as navigating a currency desert – you use whatever resources you find to reach the oasis. History shows us this isn't niche; during tough times like debt crises, a significant chunk of global trade has relied on these workarounds.

Cracking Open Locked Doors: Ever tried to sell something in a market that really, really wants to protect its own? Countertrade, especially those "offset" deals often seen in defense or aerospace, can be the key. A government might say, "Sure, we'll buy your expensive planes, if you build a factory here, train our people, or buy $X million worth of our local products." For the seller, it's a costly hoop to jump through, but it might be the only way to land that massive contract. The legendary Pepsi-for-Soviet-vodka deal wasn't just about thirst; it was Pepsi's ingenious, if unconventional, ticket into a closed-off superpower.

Finding a Home for the Unloved: Got a warehouse full of products that are perfectly fine but just... not selling for cash? Maybe they're last season's model, or slightly below top-tier quality. Countertrade offers a potential escape route, a way to swap that surplus for something more useful, turning a potential write-off into some kind of value.

Hedging Your Bets: In shaky economic climates, where a buyer might default or their currency could plummet overnight, swapping goods for goods can feel safer than waiting for a payment that might never arrive. It's a form of built-in, albeit clunky, insurance.

Okay, But What's the Catch? The Case Against the Clunkiness

While countertrade can be a clever problem-solver, economists often wince. Why? Because it throws sand in the gears of smooth commerce.

The Sheer Headache Factor: This isn't just inefficient; it's expensive inefficiency.

"What's this really worth?" Agreeing on the value of goods being swapped is a minefield. It's like trying to agree if your slightly used bike is worth their vintage record collection – subjectivity reigns, and arguments flare.

Endless Haggling: Forget quick deals. Countertrade negotiations can drag on forever, involving complex details about product quality, delivery schedules, and who's responsible for what.

The Unwanted Baggage: Often, companies end up receiving goods they have absolutely no use for. Now they need specialists or trading houses to offload these items, usually at a discount, adding yet another layer of cost and complexity. Think of it as getting paid in furniture when you needed groceries – now you have to sell the couch!

Warping the Market: Free markets work best when prices reflect true supply and demand. Countertrade messes with this. Prices might be artificially inflated or deflated to make a deal work, potentially hiding subsidies or allowing companies to dump products below cost. When governments demand offset deals, they might choose a supplier based on the goodies offered on the side, not necessarily because they have the best or cheapest primary product. Competition gets skewed.

Secrets and Shadows: These deals are often cooked up behind closed doors. This lack of transparency makes it hard to know if someone's getting a fair shake and, worryingly, opens the door to corruption, especially when massive government contracts are involved. Murky deals can hide kickbacks or politically motivated favoritism.

Playing Rough with the Rulebook: While the World Trade Organization (WTO) doesn't have a giant "NO COUNTERTRADE" sign, some practices can clash with its core principles of treating all trading partners equally and not discriminating against foreign goods. If a government forces countertrade in a way that unfairly favors local products or specific partners, it's bending, if not breaking, the rules designed for a level playing field.

The Reality: A World of Compromise

So, countertrade isn't going away anytime soon. It tends to surge when economies are stressed, when sanctions bite (think nations trading oil for food when cash is blocked), or in sectors like defense where governments pull the strings (India's offset policies are a prime example, fueling debate about whether the local benefits outweigh the costs).

Ultimately, countertrade lives in the messy middle ground between textbook free trade and the often-harsh realities of global economics and politics. It's a tool born of necessity, a "plan B" when "plan A" (cash) fails. It solves real problems – bridging currency gaps, forcing market entry – but at a cost. It's less efficient, murkier, and potentially distorts the very markets it operates in. Its continued existence is a potent reminder that the global economy isn't always the smooth, rational machine we imagine, but a complex ecosystem where survival instincts and political pressures often force creative, if less-than-perfect, solutions. The debate isn't just academic; it's about how we navigate the inevitable friction points in a deeply interconnected, yet often unequal, world.

About Author

S.A.U. Haque, with a decade in academic writing, authored many technical books and now focuses on sharing knowledge globally.

www.ingramcontent.com/pod-product-compliance
Lightning Source LLC
Chambersburg PA
CBHW031349230926
51848CB00002B/455
9783384589026